A PRIMER

**to talk about race &
dialogue across identity divisions**

A PRIMER

to talk about race &

dialogue across identity divisions

DR. KARLA D. SCOTT

© 2023 Dr. Karla Scott

ALL RIGHTS RESERVED.

No part of this book may be reproduced or transmitted in any form or by any means, electronic or mechanical, including photocopying and recording, or in any information storage or retrieval system without the prior written permission of Dialogue, Diversity, & Dharma, LLC

www.drkarladscott.com

BOOK DESIGN BY Kevin Barrett Kane
COVER ILLUSTRATION BY Jasmine Wright

Check yo stuff first published:

International Review of Qualitative Research, Vol. 11, No. 2, Summer 2018, pp. 198–209. ISSN 1940-8447, eISSN 1940-8455. © 2018 International Institute for Qualitative Research, University of Illinois, Urbana-Champaign. All rights reserved.

For my CamiBear,

May your journey be smooth.

TABLE OF CONTENTS

Introduction 1

PART ONE
**Understand the Backstory If You Want to
Learn More to Do Different** 11

Chapter One
**The Communication Model as a Process
of Human Interaction** 13
    Reflection: The Process Involves "Humans" 19
    Backstory Bag© Race 23

Chapter Two
**Curiosity: What Do We Bring to Interaction?
Identity and Our Stuff** 25
    Reflection: Learn to Be Who and How I Am 31

Chapter Three
Courage to Explore Identity, Privilege, and "Othering" 40
    White Supremacy Iceberg 46

Chapter Four
**Communicating Anti-Blackness in the Backstory:
Dismantling Takes Courage** 55
    Conclusion for Part One 77

PART TWO
Commitment to support real transformation 83

Introduction to Part Two
Commitment to Support Real Transformation 85
    Check yo' stuff! 91

Chapter Five
Active listening 102
    Listening Activity 107

Chapter Six
Language Matters: Microaggressions, and Tone Policing 110

Chapter Seven
Verbal and Nonverbal Communication Strategies for dialogue 123

Chapter Eight
What Now, What Next? Practice Compassion and Proceed with Care 129

Bibliography 139
Resources 141
Acknowledgments 147
About the Author 151

INTRODUCTION

THIS BOOK, and the class I developed from it, is a "Primer" offered as a first step on a journey to build your ability and capacity to communicate about and across racial differences and identity divisions. You may ask, "Why a Primer?" In response to your question, I pose one as well: **Have you ever taken a class that helped you improve your communication about race or across racial divisions?** I'll give you a minute to think but I find most people don't need much time because they immediately say "No, I have never learned how to talk about racial differences or divisions—in fact, I was taught not to talk about race at all." I've also found that many people do want to "do different" and "do better" when it comes to talking about race, but they don't know how or where to begin. This is why I decided to write this Primer and develop a class using it as a guide.

After more than thirty years of experience teaching in university classrooms, facilitating dialogues across campus and in organizational settings, I can give you only one thing I know for sure: There are no hacks to make this easier. If your goal is to learn more so you can engage in hard discussions that can lead to action needed right now to transform racial divisions, heal long held hurts and end the dehumanization of people considered inferior, less than, and deviant—dialogue is a specific form of communication offering that opportunity. As you begin that journey, I think it is helpful to have what I conceive of as a Primer to introduce you to key elements, concepts and language that will support your learning.

> So before answering the specific question "why a Primer," I point out how difficult it is to communicate about and across race and racial divisions because most of us have no experience doing it in a way that leads to better understanding.

So why a ***Primer?*** In the following two examples I offer further explanation:

1. *...**a Primer:** (**rhymes with skimmer**) is a first textbook for the teaching of reading—also used more broadly to refer to any book that presents the **most basic elements** of any subject.* For example, the first book I was given in my first grade reading class was about Dick, Jane, and Sally, who appeared to be siblings and their pets, Spot the dog, and Puff the cat. The first words in the book were minimal: See Dick, See Jane, See Dick run, See Jane run, Funny Sally, here Spot, etc.—just simple words accompanying the colorful pictures of them. Some of you who share my demographic may recall that across three different books or primers their adventures got more complicated and included more words. This is how we progressed at reading. And I do realize this was the early-to-mid 1960s and methods to teach reading have changed since then, but this demonstrates for me what preparation with basic elements looks like.[1]

2. *... a paint **Primer (rhymes with climber)** or undercoat is a **preparatory** coating put on materials before **painting**... ensures better adhesion of **paint** to the surface and increases **paint** durability.* In many home renovation projects, you are encouraged to start with a paint primer before you apply the carefully chosen color to your walls or floors or furniture, so the outcome is what you envisioned.

So regardless of how we pronounce it, both are examples of an

---

[1] My love for books and learning to read began with the adventures of Dick, Jane and Sally set in the mid 20th century where I saw no characters in the Primers who looked like me—a little Black girl. Representation did not matter in that cultural context but despite that reality I continued to read as much as I could. As I write this now 60 years later, I am certain there will be readers who have never considered how that lack of representation in their early education may have influenced what they have continued to learn and how they've experienced life.

emphasis on *basic elements to prepare for next steps and further work.* This intentional process at the beginning creates a solid foundation and helps lead to a more positive, productive outcome—whether it is your ability to read and comprehend or enjoy the beautiful new colors on your living room walls or refurbished antique automobile.

In the case of race, racism, and anti-Blackness in the U.S.—with divisions so long, deep, and painful—it is necessary to examine, "how we got here" to move forward—as individuals, as organizations, and as a society. This Primer provides the key basic elements for your learning; it is a starting point to build your capacity to

1. engage in individual, organizational, and societal communication to dismantle systems and structures of exclusion and oppression that devalue, denigrate, and dehumanize other human beings.

2. participate in dialogue to support better understanding across and about identity differences and divisions.

And please note that in no way do I imply with this Primer that the complexities of race in the United States (or globally) can be fully understood in one book or one course—that learning is an ongoing, lifelong process. The educational system in the United States was designed to keep us from understanding the socially constructed concept of race and the system built on it—a system structured to support racism, power, and privilege. My goal with this Primer is to offer insight and support as you begin that process of unlearning and relearning.

The first four chapters in Part One of the Primer will offer what I call a backstory to understand race and racial divisions, or *"how we got here."* As a communication scholar interested in how race, gender, class, and language influence our everyday lives, I've always said it is important to know how we got here—with *"here"* being as individuals, or as members of a small group, family, organization, or society. Backstory helps us understand the current context of our interactions—why we do what we do. As the focus on race, racism, and the protests for racial justice in the United States (and globally) continue to grow louder and larger, it is important to understand *"how we got here."* And a big part of that understanding is realizing that ***you*** are a part of how and why racial inequalities exist and persist in a larger society. Yes, individuals make up society—so to change the systems and structures that support racism and inequities, individuals must change what they think and do and how they behave in personal interactions, organizations, and in society at large to understand their own role in *"how we got here."*

Society at large is what I also call the current cultural context and that too has a backstory that has influenced our individual backstory. So how did individual actions, interactions, and behaviors build the systems of racism and inequality that have existed for centuries? That is the larger backstory of "how we got here" and it will help you to better understand what needs to be changed, and how systems can be "dismantled"—a word you may have heard often since the racial protests of 2020 grew larger and louder. Just as systems were built by individual actions they must be dismantled by individual actions—if you really want change, you can't sit on the sidelines and watch, you must act and do different if you want to do better.

Part two of this Primer offers specific communication strategies and skills that will help you to engage in dialogue to better understand "how we got here" and what you can do to create change. You cannot ignore or excuse the way you communicate if you want to be a part of the change. Communication is a process of human interaction and you need to think about what you bring to interactions about race and across identity divisions. This includes how well you listen (or not), how language matters, and how you can create real connection across divisions with the words you use. The communication skills and strategies for dialogue you learn in this part of the Primer can help you more clearly understand what is means to "do different" as an individual and how you can "do better" to help support change in larger society.

OK, take a moment and take a breath.

If this introduction to what you will find in this book makes you uncomfortable, please know this is not uncommon and you are not alone. I operate under no illusions that this is easy work in any classroom, professional context, or in any community of people. There will be those who defend, deflect, object, oppose, resist, run, and stick with their story no matter what. For example, in summer 2021, Critical Race Theory—an area of scholarship that has been a part of academic culture for decades—made its way into everyday language with accusations that revealing systemic anti-Blackness in the United States was promoting untruths and creating a false narrative. We will talk more about that later but for now I want to note how Critical Race Theory has been miscommunicated by many who do not understand it and are throwing it into the conversation as another way "liberals" and "those on the left" just want to revise history and create "pain and shame for white children" in school. This interpretation is not true, but those of us doing this work for decades are not surprised at this reaction and resistance.

Hearing information about race and racial injustice creates not just discomfort when realizing you were taught untruths, but also requires you accept you learned from well-meaning people who loved you and had your best interests at heart. Parents, grandparents, aunts, uncles, teachers, clergy, coaches, professors, mentors, the educational system, the church, the legal system, the media, social media, and language use are all part of the construction and support of a story of race that does not reflect reality.

And as you begin to realize these were lies you learned it can create discomfort. We will talk more about this process of socialization in Chapter two.

After the realization comes reconciling the untruths you were told with the role those well-meaning adults played in your life. One way to do that is to remember those who taught you were socialized in a particular cultural context as well—and depending on your demographic some of them may have learned from parents who were still participating in legal racial segregation and dehumanization of individuals living with certain social identities—think Jim Crow laws that legalized Black people being treated as inferior and less human well into the mid 1960s. Yes, it can be difficult to do different even if you know something may not be what you perceive as best.

But I hope discomfort or fear is not a reason for you to stop reading or decide that helping to transform society is something others should do—because it's just too hard to unlearn, relearn and do different in your daily life. This Primer offers the opportunity to learn more about social identities, anti-Blackness and injustice and provides specific communication strategies for dialogue that builds better understanding— and yes, that is hard. I was being honest when I said there are no hacks but this Primer does offer guidance and support as you begin your journey. Reading it comes with a big ask—a huge ask—that you sit with it, breathe through your discomfort, and engage with the information offered. My work over three decades has identified those who

> Parents, grandparents, aunts, uncles, teachers, clergy, coaches, professors, mentors, the educational system, the church, the legal system, the media, social media, and language use are all part of the construction and support of a story of race that does not reflect reality.

find it most useful on their journey to embrace and live out four critical qualities for transformation of self and society: **curiosity, courage, commitment, and compassion**.

These four concepts—the Four "Cs"—are the closest I come to offering hacks to help you with what can be a steep learning curve requiring you do serious work. As you read through the Primer, reflecting on the content and your reaction it is helpful to engage the Four "Cs" in difficult moments to keep you on the path.

CURIOSITY

As you encounter the information in this Primer, welcome **curiosity**, by asking questions such as:

1. Why are identity differences and racial divisions such a big topic right now?

2. Why are those with different racial identities treated differently and unequally?

3. Why did I not know more about the backstory of race in the U.S. and globally?

4. Where and how can I learn more?

COURAGE

Have the **courage** to continue even when the going gets rough by being mindful of:

1. What am I feeling when I encounter information that answers my questions.

2. Learning new information and unlearning what we believed is challenging and uncomfortable.

3. When you feel what you identify as fear—acknowledge it, exhale, and as bravely and gently as you can, move through it.

4. Resist the impulse to defend, defer or deflect.

COMMITMENT

This is not "one and done" work—you need to stay committed and recommit often.

1. Learning more about identity and racial divisions and how to communicate about and across them is an ongoing journey.

2. You must be mindful of your thoughts, words, actions, and reactions daily, even minute by minute.

3. Like any effort to learn something new, to do different, and to be better, reflective practice on your efforts is an important part of that process.

COMPASSION

This is not easy work and giving grace is important.

1. Forgive yourself for not knowing what you were not taught.

2. Unlearning and relearning is hard; offer grace to yourself on your journey.

3. Offer grace to others in the process as well.

4. Dismantling injustice and "isms" can cause a particular form of fatigue, remember to practice restorative care to support your well-being.

You may have noticed, in discussing these Four "Cs" of curiosity, courage, commitment, and compassion, that I've made multiple references to mindfulness and restorative care. That's because this learning process in which we are now engaging is not just intellectual. For many readers, if not most, this work will probably pull deeply upon your emotions and cause you to think more deeply about the stories and social context in which you were raised and are living in now. Some of the work you do will be with me here on the pages of this Primer, but this work, if you take it up, will also continue in the busy and the quiet moments of your life. And in these moments, taking the time to notice what and how you are feeling, to notice what is arising in your mind, your emotions, and your body will help you metabolize, process, and transform your relationship to these concepts. And so, I do recommend and, in fact, see the need for reflective practice as part of this journey of re-educating not simply the mind, but the heart.

As I conclude this introduction you might find yourself asking another question: **Who is the audience for this Primer?** My answer is anyone! Yes, I have written this Primer and developed a course for anyone who wants to know *"how we got here"* and what can we do to do better? And by *"here"* I mean:

1. **Why** we can't communicate about racial differences and identity divisions in ways that lead to real understanding that supports transformation.

2. **Why** the concept of Critical Race Theory has frightened so many across the country that laws are being passed to ensure educators who want to "do different and do better" by offering information that includes more than just a white supremacist narrative cannot do so in their classrooms because it will "evoke shame" in white school children, their parents, caregivers, and even other educators.

3. **Why** the January 6, 2021, attack on the United States Capitol was allowed to happen even though government social media surveillance revealed plans for the violent, illegal activity there was little effort to prevent it.

But "**here**" is also the moment when many do want to know more and discover information that was withheld not just in their education in the U.S. but as they grew up in, and were socialized into families, communities, and even religious institutions. "**Here**" *in the Primer is where encountering basic elements and concepts can lead to further learning and support doing different.*

As we cover the content in the Primer you will begin to see how the information, encountering new knowledge and skills, and embracing the Four "Cs" will help prepare you for dialogue that makes a difference.

It is the closest I can come to a "hack." I hope that together with this Primer as a guide we can explore how you can discover and further develop skills in each area and depend on them as you begin your journey to "do different" and "do better" in your communication about and across race and identity divisions. This is the foundation for dialogue that builds better understanding.

PART ONE

UNDERSTAND THE BACKSTORY IF YOU WANT TO LEARN MORE TO DO DIFFERENT

CHAPTER ONE

THE COMMUNICATION MODEL AS A PROCESS OF HUMAN INTERACTION

HAVE YOU EVER TAKEN a course on how to communicate? Not one focused on how to use technology or even one that shares secrets to connecting with your beloved pet. I mean a course that helped you to better understand what goes on in the process of human beings interacting in what is called communication. To better understand the importance of racial differences, social identity divisions and how to dialogue across them we begin with a chapter that examines what happens in that interaction and the communication elements in that process.

If you have never taken a communication class, please know you are not alone. In my more than thirty years of teaching in university classrooms and training sessions for organizations I have had very few students who have had such a class. Many have taken public speaking and shared that in that class they learned something about connecting with others when developing a specific form of a speech. But beyond how to present information in an organized, coherent form—written or verbal—very few learn what is involved in the actual process of human communication. And yes, I will continue to emphasize **HUMAN** communication because that is important to remember—humans are complex, complicated beings with emotions, perceptions, fears, and faults and we all became who and how we are through a process of identity socialization.

We all bring to any human communication process "who and how we are" and those experiences of living "who and how we are"—or what I call **"stuff"**—does not always allow us to understand the other in the communication process who is also bringing "who and how they are" because of their **stuff**.

> What we learned in that process of becoming "who and how we are" also created our beliefs and assumptions that we know exactly how someone else is going to act and react in a human communication encounter. But we cannot guarantee that will be true.

Sit with that a moment.

We will return to the concept of **stuff** shortly. As we work our way toward a longer discussion of what this stuff looks like, it is helpful share a definition of communication and examine the elements of the process of human interaction.

DEFINITION OF COMMUNICATION

For many years I have used an efficient definition of human communication as ***the process of creating shared meaning of symbols.*** There are many other definitions—some longer and more complex—that you can find to help you better understand the process, but for inclusion in our Primer, I like the simplicity of this definition. What I appreciate most in this definition is it highlights a **process** or an act of *doing something*—and the doing is "creating shared meaning of symbols." So, you might ask, "how hard is that?" You come together with another human, or several humans, heck, even a large group of humans, and you talk, and you listen—how hard can that be—right?

Yes, it does seem like it is that is easy. But if you look at the Transactional Model of Communication in figure 1, a visual representing the elements of the process, you can start to understand why it is not that easy. Also note that transactional indicates ongoing, so while a communicator is sending a message, they are also receiving a message from the other communicator—in the form of feedback to that message.

If we take a closer look at each of the elements of the human communication process it starts to become clear why this process is more complex than most of us believe.

Sender: One who transmits a message.

Message: The idea a sender wants to convey. It is in the message that shared meaning of symbols is created but that can be complicated by the two types of "meaning":

1. content meaning and

2. relationship meaning of a message. (An example of this is in the discussion of cultural context below)

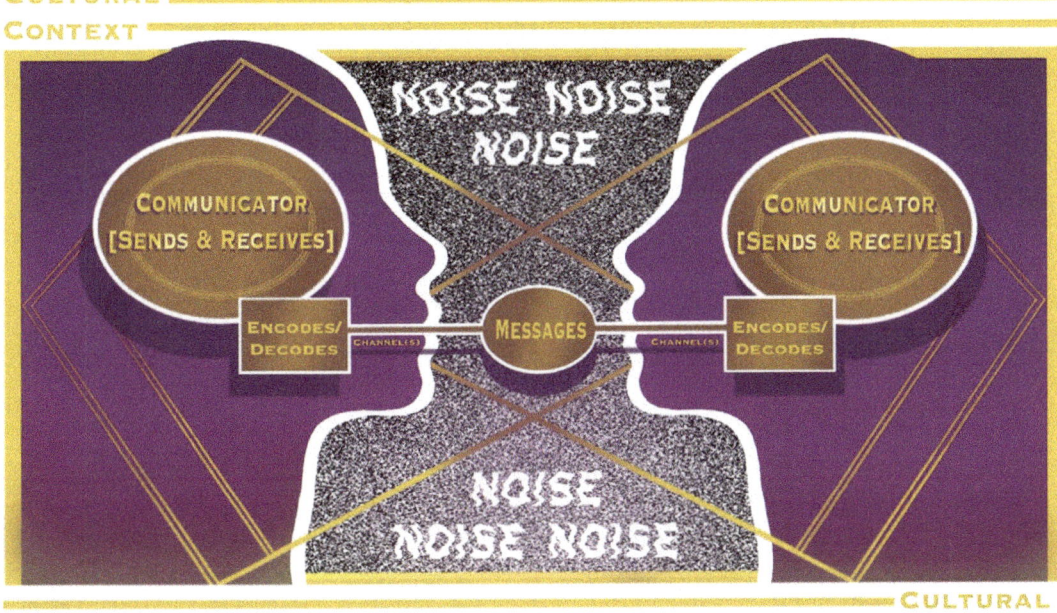

© Paris Sharp

Encoding: The selection of certain words or other symbols to express an idea.

Channel: The method (verbal, nonverbal, written, oral) used to deliver a message.

Receiver: Any person who notices and attaches some meaning to a message.

Decoding: Making sense of the words or other symbols received—including feedback about the message sent.

Noise: Factors that interfere with the exchange of messages and creation of shared meaning—physical and psychological forms.

Cultural context: Conditions and circumstances in which the message being sent such as: time of day, who are the communicators, place, space, the others "in the room" when it occurs and yes, even specific periods in larger social and historical settings. The cultural context is also where the concept of power becomes obvious in the message and meaning making—for example when one communicator has more power than the other, "shared meaning" of a message may not be possible due to the relationship—this is what is noted above in the message definition. For example, you might be sharing a meal with someone who asks for salt. The content is the request for the salt and the way it is communicated can indicate the relationship of the communicator to the one responding to the request. Is it a polite request, or a demand? Does it come with an expectation that the person responding is solely responsible for providing and cannot object or resist the request? It is quite possible to realize how a relationship is revealed in communication but often overlooked. The cultural context can also include non-verbal cues such as body language, gestures, the tone of voice and eye contact.

Why is it important to identify the elements of communication?

1. It helps to emphasize the outcome of the process is a shared meaning of the message.
   » Is that always as easy as illustrated in the model?
   » What about when participants have different lived experiences?

2. Examining the elements also emphasizes that it is ***human interaction;*** it involves people and we each have experiences from our everyday lives that we bring with us to the process of human communication. Those experiences may be similar to the experiences of others with whom we interact, but many of our experiences may be different.

Here is an example:

What do you call a non-alcoholic, flavored carbonated beverage?

Soda?   Pop?   Coke?

Depending on the area of the United States—or even the world, it can have different names. Yes, a geographical experience can create a different understanding of just a beverage. (*Shout out and much love to my Chicago cousins—the Grahams for this childhood lesson when they would visit in my southern Illinois hometown of East St. Louis. Their use of the word "pop" rather than "soda" gave me early insight into the complexity of language and sparked a curiosity about words and worlds that remains with me today.*) This is a very lighthearted and benign example, but think about the other ways differences in lived experiences may make it hard to have shared meaning of much more abstract concepts such as: **justice, wellness, or even love**?

> And what about someone whose lived experiences in a specific cultural context did not even include asking for or drinking such a beverage? Again, the same can be true for those whose lived experiences and cultural contexts challenge a shared understanding of critical concepts in human interaction such as justice, wellness, and love—for those living with histories of discrimination and prejudice and have been treated as less than or not fully human "justice" may be more of an abstract concept they have not experienced in their own life or community.

A CASE STUDY ON THE LACK OF COMMUNICATION

A mother says to her teenage child "No, you're not going anywhere with your friends until you clean your room. It's time for you to take me seriously when I say you must clean up after yourself and the messes you make. Look at this room, your clothes are on the floor, they don't belong there do they? There is trash everywhere, I even see dirty dishes and it smells like a garbage can. Did something die in here? You will have to clean up and take care of this mess before you can go have fun." An hour later as she sits in the kitchen on her computer, her teen comes into the room and says "It's done."

They go to the room together, the floor is clear of clothes, but they are all piled on the bed, trash has been placed in a small trashcan that is overflowing but pressed down to keep it flat.

And the dirty dishes are stacked on the desk by the door. The mother turns to her teen and asks: "Is this what clean up after yourself means to you?"

So, ask yourself in this example:

WHAT HAPPENED TO SHARED MEANING?

WHICH COMMUNICATION ELEMENTS CONTRIBUTED TO THE OUTCOME?

If you work through the following activity it can help with better understanding how the elements of communication can complicate the process of human interaction.

REFLECTION

THE PROCESS INVOLVES "HUMANS"

IT MIGHT HELP if you think about an example where you believe communication failed. Think of a specific context for communication, such as the one shared above, maybe with family members, or in your workplace, a community gathering, school, social organization you belong to. Where do you think the communication process and "shared meaning" can be challenged? Maybe you have an example of this.

Select three of the elements of the communication process and describe briefly how the meeting in the middle for "shared meaning"—can be complicated, difficult or might not happen at all using examples of the elements as discussed in the previous section.

Use the space below for your response. You may have a different example for each of the three elements or you may be able to use one example for all three elements. If you don't have actual examples, again think of how the various elements might interfere with the process of creating shared meaning.

1. _____
_____
_____
_____
_____
_____

2. _____
_____
_____
_____
_____
_____
_____

3. _____
_____
_____
_____
_____
_____
_____

The elements of the communication process make it challenging to find shared meaning of symbols across different identities because those identities include the stuff we bring to any encounter. As a result, we receive, perceive, and make sense of symbols differently.

How often have you encountered this image that asks if you see an old woman or young woman? If you see only one image initially it is hard to visualize the other—I've had some students who can never see the other image. For many of us over time it becomes easier to see the other image. If this is your first time, who do you see—an old or young woman?

The Old/Young Woman image is another fun example to share and talk about and while it obviously has little to do with our socialization and stuff it does illustrate how we all don't see the same thing even though we see the same thing. And that is true in the process of human communication as well. Why and how do we encounter a concept, phenomenon, or another human being and not have shared meaning of what is happening?

BACKSTORY

I believe this happens because we all have a backstory that is part of our stuff, and it is what we bring to each interaction and influences what we perceive, believe, and act on when we communicate. Where did you get the stuff you bring to the process of human interaction? It happens in a very specific form of communication called socialization—it is where we learn who and how we are—and who and how we are not. This process creates our identities as we move through our everyday experiences with other humans.

Before we discuss the process of socialization let's look at some of the stuff you are bringing to communication across identity differences and racial divisions. **The Backstory Bag**© activity will prompt you to think about how and maybe where you got your stuff and how it influences interaction today. Take some time to complete the activity and in Chapter 2 we will talk more about the process of identity socialization.

BACKSTORY BAG© INSTRUCTIONS & REFLECTION

On the left side of the bag are packing cubes—label at least 2 cubes with racial identities—your own and one other. Imagine that inside each cube are messages about those identities you heard at points in your life from various sources. The cubes are different sizes to contain different amounts—and if you think one cube is not big enough for all the messages you received from all sources, then please use multiple cubes.

On the right side of the bag "unpack" each cube to reveal memorable messages you recall about your own racial identity and other racial identities. As you unpack you can depict messages any way you choose—in words, images, emojis, even perhaps a short story. *This is your stuff.*

As you reflect on your Backstory Bag© **record the answers to the following questions:**

1. How does the stuff on the right side of the bag influence your communication *across and about racial* differences?
   _____
   _____
   _____
   _____

BACKSTORY BAG© RACE

On the left side of the bag are packing cubes—label at least 2 cubes with racial identities: your own and one other. Imagine that inside each cube are messages about those identities you heard at points in your life from various sources. The cubes are different sizes to contain different amounts—and if you think one cube is not big enough for all the messages you received from all sources, please use multiple cubes.

On the right side of the bag, "unpack" the cubes to reveal memorable messages about your own and other racial identities.

This is your "stuff." Depict messages you received any way you choose: words, images, emojis, etc.

How does the "stuff" on the right side of the bag influence your communication *across and about* racial differences?
How does it contribute to positive outcomes in these interactions?
How does it contribute to negative outcomes?
How long have you had this stuff?
What can you let go of?

© Dr. Karla D. Scott DDDLLC – All rights reserved

2. How does it contribute to positive/productive outcomes in these interactions?
   _____
   _____

3. How does it contribute to more negative/nonproductive outcomes?
   _____
   _____

4. How long have you had this stuff?
   _____
   _____

5. What can you let go of?
   _____
   _____

As you make time to sit with this activity and reflect on what you might have discovered about your own backstory, the stuff in your bag and how long you've been "rolling with it," remember this is what you bring to any human interaction about racial differences and across identity divisions. It shows up in the process of communication depicted in the model at the beginning of this chapter. It can be in the words the sender used, the encoding or decoding, the channel—verbal or nonverbal or it can be noise showing up as bias, prejudice and even hate. And stuff is most certainly influenced by cultural context—when you consider how the interaction is occurring in a specific time, place, and even location that supports the need to hold onto your stuff because there is a fear of letting it go. This is where reflecting on the Four "Cs", especially curiosity and courage, might help you find information that can help you to replace beliefs you've had about "them" and "those people" with information and ideas that is not only more accurate but also affirms their humanity.

In the next chapter we will discuss more about how we are socialized into our own identities and our beliefs about other identities. This is where curiosity can help you as you think about the importance of identity in human interaction and how the stuff we bring influences communication about racial differences and across divisions—and can impact the outcome.

CHAPTER TWO

CURIOSITY: WHAT DO WE BRING TO INTERACTION? IDENTITY AND OUR STUFF

AS YOU READ the title of this chapter, I hope it sparks *curiosity* that motivates you to want to know more about how your identity and your stuff may influence your participation in the process of communication. My goal with this chapter is to help you explore and better understand how the outcomes of communication are created by the communicators interacting with the communication elements in the process.

One of my favorite discussions of interpersonal communication or relational communication is the metaphor Loraine Halfen Zephyr and communication theorist Sam Keltner coined the "Spiritual Child" to describe what occurs when two people come together in a relationship. In this connection they give birth to a "Spiritual Child" that requires continued care and nurturing to thrive in good health. I discovered this metaphor early in my graduate program in the book, *Bridges Not Walls: A book about interpersonal communication* by John Stewart (1986) and it helped me to better understand that relationships develop as they do because of what we each bring to interaction, and in that process of interaction, the spirit of the relationship or a "Spiritual Child" is created and continues to live as we nurture it. What was also eye-opening for me in this metaphor is that the child continues to live as long as one of the communicators is alive—yes, we can still interact with the memories of that other person and our experiences with them and continue to nurture the good health of the child—or not.

The Spiritual Child is what is created in the space between communicators—and through the process that is their communication—and the quality of the spirit of the relationship, or the Spiritual Child's life is determined through interaction. Zephyr writes:

> If we come together in care, authenticity, honesty, and positive regard, our child will be healthy, vibrant, winsome, and beautiful. We will love it, will receive much joy in the nurturing of it and will be nourished in return. If our child is created in dishonesty, exploitation, contempt, disregard, our child will be sickly…toxic, frustrated. It will be ugly. We will fly from it, abandon it, but its influence will linger (Stewart, 1983, 34).

Zephyr recommends that to make healthy spiritual children we must be straight with ourselves and honest with others. Having a curiosity about learning is critical in that process to appreciate who and how we are in moments of interaction and communication. If the child is not healthy, we need to ask why and, just as one would with a child with physical injuries and wounds, ask "what can I do to help healing occur?"

I believe the Spiritual Child metaphor can help us better understand how we got "here" in individual, societal, and institutional interactions about race, across identity differences, and especially racial divisions. We have not come to these interactions with honesty, and we haven't been curious enough to seek the truth. The history of racism communicated through interaction is fueled by negative disregard and beliefs about "those people" being less than, not worthy and in the case of anti-Blackness not even human. This unhealthy energy, food, or substance is what has nurtured–or in some instances poisoned—human interaction about and across race and identity differences for centuries. The result is a "Spiritual Child" that cannot be healthy. Zephyr does, however, offer strategies to "do different" to achieve healthier children and it begins with self-reflection. Again, reflective practice is where it is possible to better understand what you bring and what you should release to move forward. If you completed the Backstory Bag© activity you should have some insight about what you bring—and even where you got your stuff. In this next section we will talk a bit more about how that happens.

Becoming who and how we are occurs through a process of socialization. It occurs when we receive messages from senders, and in the process of encoding and decoding we learn about ourselves, others, and the world we live in. As a result of the ongoing communication, we develop identities—yes more than one—and we learn not just who we are, and are not, but also how we are to behave, what to believe and what our interaction with other humans should be like.

Think of how we see newborns, in the beginning of life, they are indeed a "blank slate" or as I recall from my introduction to philosophy class a "tabula rasa" which is Latin for blank slate (and yes, I realize this is an oversimplification). But at the beginning of life humans have no prejudices, stereotypes, or biases toward other humans. In fact, a favorite social media meme is of little children with what appears to be various racial identities playing happily together, hugging with a caption reminding us racism and hatred is learned. In our early socialization experiences learning begins through our communication with family, friends, extended relatives, caregivers, those we know, love and trust. From those early experiences we encounter norms, values, roles, rules and start to learn not just who we are to be but *how we are to be*. In communication from institutions and cultural communities the learning continues. Think of the messages you received during your education, as a member of religious communities, what you learned from the media—and social media—and may have encountered in the legal systems. Even the language used by humans in our everyday experiences communicates more than just the information we want to share—it can also influence how we see ourselves and others. (Remember the content and relationship aspects of messages?). And it is important to note here that the messages of socialization are constant, conscious and unconscious, and cumulative. Yes, they are ongoing, and we are not even aware of what we are communicating or what is being communicated to us.

For example, in the second wave women's movement of the 1970s, calls for the use of gender-neutral language began to grow louder as the historic use of a generic "he" to mean all humans was condemned for lack of representing women as participants outside of traditionally accepted feminine roles and excluding them as fully human. A former student of mine remembers reading a social studies text in the late 1970s, which referenced "the citizen, he." She recalled how she had to reread the sentence several times before it dawned on her, "oh that he means everyone." She is now a teacher, and she often shares this with her students who have grown up with more inclusive classroom materials. Students in the current cultural context don't have to stop and question whether the designation of citizen includes them.

Another strategy developed during that mid-century period to affirm the full humanity of women was the use of Ms. as a title that de-emphasized the relationship of a woman to a man, whether her father or husband. Prior to the introduction of Ms. the titles used exclusively were Miss if unmarried and Mrs. if married.

One thing most of us do know, however, is that if we respond to the messages we receive (consciously or unconsciously) and willingly comply with the beliefs and expectations; they become part of our everyday experiences and we are rewarded for compliance, for "being good little children." As we grow into adulthood, we see that complying can be empowering, and offer privileges. Sadly, we can also discover that if we don't comply to what we are being socialized to become, we can be punished, stigmatized, and persecuted. As a result of this socialization that we aren't often aware of, we can live without objection to the messages and happily embrace our identities and the beliefs, behaviors and expectations of them. And it is also true that sometimes we may resist or reject them and work to redefine who and how we are. And this can happen when we start to realize that what we were taught and what we learned is not how we want to be in the world any longer—embracing an identity as an "us" that relies on biased beliefs when interacting with others we were taught are "them." Often this happens when we find the process of human interaction has changed because the context in which it occurs has changed—for example when children leave home to attend college, join the military or start their own families.

Remember all communication occurs in a context—more specifically in a **cultural context** of humans interaction. This includes a specific time, specific place/location—think country, environment, institution, and the communicators participating in the process—or in the room where it happens. And this is true for socialization as well; we become who and how we are—**and are not**—in a particular context that is also a cultural context.

MY OWN GENDER SOCIALIZATION IN THE CULTURAL CONTEXT OF 1969

For many years I called myself a "tail-end baby boomer" born almost at the cut off for that generation but still growing up very much with the influence. In early 2022, I discovered a more accurate title is Generation Jones for those born between 1954 and 1965. When I was about 11 or 12 my older brother, male cousins and a couple of their friends had what would be today called a "garage band." Though we had no garages the concept was the same, they gathered in basements and bedrooms and played guitars as they learned the music of Sly and the Family Stone, Santana, Led Zeppelin, and Jimi Hendrix. One day I thought it would be cool to join them as a drummer. I recall vividly my mother—my dear Doris Jean—was in the kitchen at the sink, back to me when I said proudly, "I want to play drums" and without missing a beat she slightly turned her head over her shoulder and said without any emotion: "Girls don't play drums" and went right back to washing dishes, or cleaning vegetables. I shrugged, turned, left the kitchen, and never thought again about being a drummer. Why? Because at that time the 11-year-old, preteen me (we weren't tweens then) really didn't see any women who were drummers. It was 1969 I believe and while I am certain there were girls and women drumming somewhere I didn't see that as normal in my world; so I accepted my mother's claim because I thought she knew best—yes?

In this example of socialization, we can see how I got a message about what girls did and did not do and I did not challenge it—I saw little of that in my world as well. But today we have so many women drummers and technology allows those images to be shared across multiple platforms. If there were women rock drummers in 1968 or 1969 the only place I might have seen them was on The Ed Sullivan Show—and I don't recall him ever showcasing rock bands—though I do vividly remember the Jackson 5 debuting on his Sunday night show.

As my own story demonstrates, in the cultural context there are beliefs, biases, and behaviors that are normal for the time, place, environment, and the participants. This is where we learn about "us" and "them" and, yes, even "those people"—all done through various forms of the communication process:

1. one-on-one interpersonal, with our family,

2. in organizations and institutions,

3. and yes, through ongoing, 24/7 media and now social media messages.

These are all forms of communication with messages of socialization in a particular cultural context that influence our understanding and interpretation of what we encounter in the daily experiences of living.

REFLECTION

LEARN TO BE WHO AND HOW I AM

Take just a moment here and think about your own socialization at a specific time in your life and record your responses below:

1. What did you learn about your own identities? Race, gender, social class, religion?

   _____
   _____
   _____
   _____
   _____
   _____
   _____
   _____
   _____

2. What do you recall about the time and even your age when you received messages?

   _____
   _____
   _____
   _____
   _____
   _____
   _____
   _____
   _____

3. Who communicated messages about identity to you?

   _____
   _____
   _____
   _____
   _____
   _____
   _____
   _____

4. What was the message or messages communicated to you?

   _____
   _____
   _____
   _____
   _____
   _____
   _____
   _____

5. How did you respond to those messages?

   _____
   _____
   _____
   _____
   _____
   _____
   _____
   _____

6. Where did you see examples of others who shared your identity or identities? Or grown-up versions of people living with your identities?

   _____
   _____
   _____
   _____
   _____

_____
_____

7. What messages do you recall about them?
_____
_____
_____
_____
_____
_____
_____

Because of socialization in cultural contexts, we develop social identities. In her book *Difference Matters: Communicating Social Identity*, communication scholar Brenda J. Allen defines social identities as aspects of a person's self-image derived from group-based categories and she refers to "the ways in which individuals and collectivities are distinguished in their social relations with other individuals and collectivities" (Allen, 2011, 11). Allen says social identity matters because we routinely use social identity categories to differentiate ourselves. Those categories often are the basis for positive and negative biases and stereotypes.

Here are categories with examples of more specific ways of identifying

Age: Child, Young Adult, Middle-Aged Adult, Elderly

Ability: People with disabilities (cognitive, physical, emotional, etc.), Temporarily able-bodied, Temporarily disabled

Ethnicity: Chinese, Guatemalan, Irish, Italian, Jewish, Puerto Rican, Mohawk, Guatemalan, Lebanese, European-American

Gender: Woman, Man, Transgender, Post-Gender Sex - Intersex, Nonbinary, Female, Male

Nation(s) of Origin and/or Citizenship: United States, Nigeria, Korea, Argentina

Tribal or Indigenous Affiliation: Mohawk, Aboriginal, Navajo, Santal

Race: Asian, Bi/Multiracial, Black, Latino/a/@, Native American, Pacific Islander, White

Religion, Spirituality, Faith: Agnostic, Atheist, Buddhist, Christian, Hindu, Humanist, Jewish, Muslim, Pagan, Secular Humanist

Sexual Orientation: Bisexual, Gay, Heterosexual, Lesbian, Pan-Attractional, Asexual, Queer, Questioning

Social Cwlass: Poor, Working Class, Lower-Middle Class, Upper-Middle Class, Owning Class,

In the process of socialization, we identify as members of an identity group. And what is important to point out here is that some identities have **privilege and power**—and others have little if any. (We will talk more about this in chapter 3). The result of this socialization into an identity or identities is that individuals with power and privilege ***communicate*** in ways that construct and support their power and privilege, which sustains inequities and dehumanizes "others," perpetuating oppression.

This is how we can begin to see how identity matters in the human communication process. Up until the mid to late 20th century, the cultural context supported sending messages to those who identified as members of Black, Brown, Indigenous racial categories that they were not equal, or fully human in this process of human interaction. Jim Crow laws in the United States even made it legal to treat people of African descent as inferior. They were referred to, and treated as, "other," "those people" and "them" and communication in most forms only furthered divisions with no affirmation of humanity. Here, however, in the early 21st century, questions about what we learned in socialization about "others," "them," and "those people" have turned to protests and actions focused on how we can resist those messages, redefine perceptions, restore humanity and redesign messages to communicate equity and affirm humanity.

I believe the killing of George Floyd in May 2020 was a moment when many whites in the United States began to question what they had been told about Black men and criminal behavior as they saw a man being slowly killed while others watched and begged that his life be spared. The callous disregard of the officer was hard to ignore, and it was painful to see a human being treated this way. This questioning can also be a part of a socialization process. It is a concept known as **cognitive dissonance** which describes what happens when we encounter something, or someone that challenges our beliefs, leading us to see disagreement or motivating a decision to change our behavior—even when interacting with others who live with different identities.

In a discussion of this process of coming to greater awareness of social injustice, I refer to education scholar Bobbie Harro (2000) who notes that, at the core of this realization that what you were told is true may actually not be true, is the motive for decisions to act in a new way on a new belief. But not all who encounter new information go on to new beliefs and instead they may choose actions out of *fear, ignorance, confusion, and uncertainty*. We can certainly see how we might ask "why did I stay in this place so long, embracing messages that were wrong?" Uncertainty, says scholar Brené Brown is a vulnerable place to be, "we are in a torture chamber we call uncertainty and yes were taking on huge emotional risk when we allow ourselves to be vulnerable."

In my thirty plus years of teaching, I have witnessed these moments of cognitive dissonance as students encounter for the first time in their lives roommates, classmates, residence hall advisors, and even professors of another race. They are now having ongoing daily interaction with "them" and "those people" who they were told to avoid because they are "less than," or deficient in some way and deviant. Or they had been told "not to see race" because it doesn't matter." But with the opportunities to have continuous and frequent interaction with "them" students start to understand how their new friends and classmates of color must constantly worry about how race will impact their daily living—and can even put them at risk for dying.

Over the years, I have seen students react to this realization by taking specific classes to learn more, choosing to study abroad, joining student groups and even forming new groups—so they can support change and transformation. I have also witnessed other students who choose to ignore the realities of social injustice and do nothing—some have shared with me they find it is just too hard or the risks are not worth it. Transformation and growth are difficult decisions for many living with privileged identities and some of the reasons for resistance include guilt, reactions from family and friends, lack of awareness about implicit bias, fear of saying or doing the wrong thing, or even that they are benefitting in some way from racism. Some may think that race is no longer a big deal—after all Barack Obama was a Black man elected president of the United States, surely race no longer matters. Without interaction or close relationships with Black, Indigenous and people of color, many white people don't believe race is a problem.

For my students whose cognitive dissonance did motivate change, they pursued a path of learning that includes actions Bobbie Harro (2000) notes as: Interrupting, learning more, conscious raising groups/activities, intervening. We will talk more about those actions in the next chapters and will begin with a closer look at social identity and "othering" in the communication process.

Hearing information about race and racial injustice creates not just discomfort when realizing you were taught untruths, but also requires you accept you did not learn the truth even though the people who taught you were well-meaning people who loved you and had your best interests at heart. This can include parents, grandparents, aunts, uncles, teachers, clergy, coaches, professors, and mentors and that socialization was further supported through the educational system, the church, the legal system, media, social media and even through language. There comes a time when you have to recognize and accept that the lies you learned were not truth, and they were deliberately taught to you by those who had your best interests at heart. They were teaching you what they were taught.

Additional discomfort happens when you must then reconcile that new insight with the role those people played in your life. I suggest one way you can do that is to remember they, too, were socialized in a particular cultural context into identities. Depending on your demographic—especially your age—some of your parents may have learned from parents who were still participating in legal segregation and dehumanization of individuals living with certain social identities—after all, Jim Crow laws were in place until the early 1960s. Also remember at that time representations of members of other racial identities were limited and what was offered was often gross mischaracterizations of marginalized groups who were not in positions of power to tell their own story. Anyone recall the "Cowboy and Indian" movies popular in the mid 20th century? I remember "Picture for a Sunday afternoon" movies televised into homes each weekend where movies with white cowboys were the heroes who fought against people often called "savages" in the "wild west." In the movies most of the Indigenous characters called "Indians" were portrayed by white actors—a common practice in the movie industry. Also popular at that time were movies with Chinese Detective Charlie Chan where the main character was played by a white man made up to look as if he was of Chinese descent.

As you begin your journey to unlearn and relearn, remember who taught you about race—you learned about race and other social identities, during in a specific cultural context, and were taught by those who were socialized in another, probably different cultural context. Those people passed on what they were taught to you because they did not question what they learned—because the context did not support other perspectives. But you can now question—you can do different and do better.

As we examine identity it is important to think about how we often don't know how we show up in the world, in our interactions and in communication about and across race and identity differences. A person can think, believe, and say, "I'm not racist," but others can see differently. A concept called the Johari Window can offer an opportunity for you to reflect on how you really show up. If you take time to think about this model and complete the different areas represented, you can also begin to think about how power and privilege in identity influence communication across racial divisions. We will discuss identity, privilege, and othering further in chapter 3.

ARE YOU AWARE OF YOUR STUFF?

The Johari Window is a concept and activity frequently recommended when seeking to improve self-awareness in communication in interpersonal (one-to-one) contexts, small groups or organizational contexts. I am including it here because I believe in the larger current cultural context communication across identities and racial divisions can greatly benefit from improved self-awareness.

This model was developed in the 1950s by psychologists, Joseph Luft and Harry Ingham—combining the two first names led to the title "Johari Window." As you can see in the model there are four areas for examination—think of each of them as a pane in the window:

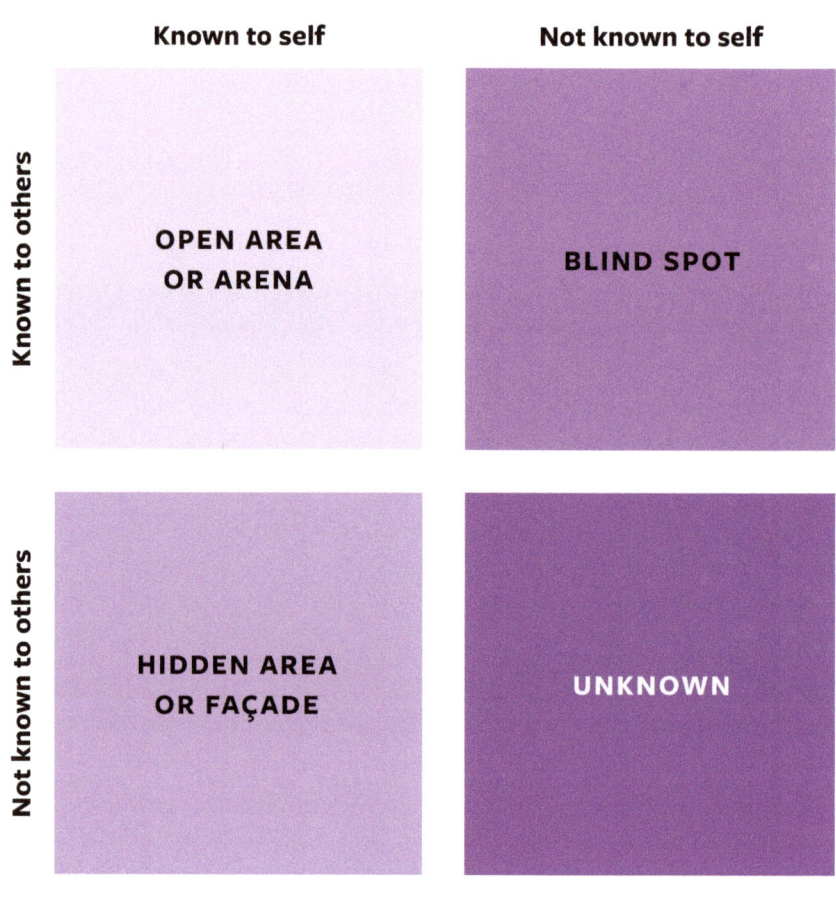

1. Open area: Known to self and others

2. Blind spot: Not known to self but known to others

3. Hidden: Known to self but not others

4. Unknown: Not known to self or others

In each of the panes of the window is our **stuff**. If we are aware of it and others are as aware as well, it's open. If there is stuff we may not want others to know, it is hidden. And the stuff we are not aware of is in the blind area. There is also the unknown stuff, or perhaps yet to be discovered area—or as I like to think, the area that can also be discovered as learning occurs about self and others in interaction.

Take some time to think about the Johari Window and each pane and record your responses below. This is another opportunity to once more think about the stuff you bring to communication about identities and across racial divisions.

1. What do you know about yourself that is open to others? What can others easily see?

2. What do you think (fear) others might know about you that you don't know?

3. What do you hide? Or keep others from discovering?

4. What do you think might be unknown now and yet to be discovered on your path to unlearning/relearning? (Obviously this is a hard one, we often don't know what we don't know but give it a try.)

CHAPTER THREE

COURAGE TO EXPLORE IDENTITY, PRIVILEGE, AND "OTHERING"

I START THIS CHAPTER with an admission, and perhaps a warning about the content you are about to encounter. For many, if not most, of the people I've worked with over three decades, the process of learning more to do different in communication about race and across identity divisions can be uncomfortable, overwhelming, and scary. Taking a deep dive into how your identity influences your experiences and how you treat others because of their identities requires courage. As we just discussed in Chapter two, we learn about our own identities and those who are different from us in the process of socialization where we interact with symbols of various identities and the messages communicated are:

"This is who you are, and this is who you are not."

"We are this and 'they' are that…."

Recall the social identities identified in the previous chapter:

Ability	Race
Age	Religion
Ethnicity	Sexual orientation
Gender	Social class
Nationality	

In this process of socialization, we identify as members of a social category with a social identity. And what we will explore further now is how some identities have privilege and power—and others have little, if any. We will take a closer look at how individuals with **power** and **privilege** communicate in ways that construct, support, and sustain inequity, dehumanize "others," and perpetuate oppression. This is possible because the socialization process creates what is often called **target** *and* **agent** identities:

1. Target identities are social identity groups that are disenfranchised and exploited in certain cultural contexts.

2. Agent identity groups are social identity groups that hold unearned privileges in certain cultural contexts.

What does this look like?

A target is:

- something or someone fired at or marked for attack.

- a goal to be achieved.

- an object of ridicule or criticism; something or someone to be affected by an action or development.

Targets do not do anything, they do not act, they are acted on.

An agent is:

- one that acts or exerts power.

- something that produces or can produce an effect.

- one who is authorized to act for or in the place of another as a representative, emissary, or official of a government crown *agent*. (Think of a **"federal agent."**)

Agents can do, they act on something or someone, they are not acted on.

Through the socialization process some individuals develop identities with *privilege and power* and others get socialized into identities with little, if any, privilege and power. And most don't recognize this as stuff they learned, embrace, enact and bring to communication in their everyday lives. More often than not, this is where implicit bias begins: Implicit bias is a concept to describe how we don't even realize that we believe _____ about "them."

Implicit bias for our discussion can be defined as negative beliefs that people unknowingly hold about other people—but bias is not only about people. We can hold implicit bias about food, art, clothing, locations, music, art, books and much more that we encounter in daily living. Bias can be expressed automatically without conscious awareness, and they affect attitudes and emotions and create real actions with real life implications. Everyone has implicit biases and what's important to keep in mind for our discussion is that often a negative bias can be revealed and it can contradict a stated positive belief about others who are not part of our ingroup. What we believe about "them" gets communicated in words, actions, practices, and policies—without knowing we are doing it.

Implicit bias is a concept to describe how we don't even realize that we believe _____ about "them."

EXAMPLE

There is research on "ethnic sounding" names on resumes of job applicants that examines how bias can operate in the employment process. On two applicants' resumes everything was identical: statement of interest, education and degree earned, same number of years of experience in the professional field, previous positions held related to the position sought. The only difference was in the name of the applicants: For example, one has a first name of Emily, the other was LaKisha. Applicants with Black names were called back ten percent fewer times across the board — and even less when it came to specific companies—despite having comparable applications to their white counterparts.

If all qualifications are identical, why would Emily be the preferred hire? What is it about the name "LaKisha"—the only difference that would keep those in the position to hire from contacting her? Is it because they believe something about someone name LaKisha, that they don't believe about Emily?

How and why is this still happening?

Obviously, this pattern has something to do with the person in the position with the power to identify potential job candidates. If we were to ask them why Emily was called and not LaKisha, I am sure it is possible this is a person who would willingly proclaim:

"I didn't even know the race of applicants and I have no racial bias or prejudice and I am certainly not racist." And ok, if that is true, given the same education and job experiences—why call Emily over LaKisha? What do you believe Emily brings that LaKisha cannot?

This is implicit bias—there is some belief about someone who has that name. What is that belief? And clearly if you are in a position to review candidates for employment that is an example of how power and privilege in a specific cultural context of an organization are communicated in ways that sustain systems of racism and oppression.

Oh, ok, yes, and there is that word—**oppression**—that you have probably heard more since the summer of 2020 Black Lives Matter protests called for a racial reckoning.

What is oppression? This is an important word to understand if you want to improve your communication about race and across identity divisions. We can define oppression as:

The exercise of authority or power in a burdensome, cruel, or unjust manner (Frye 1983).

1. So again, here is power, and the power of certain identities—agent identities, those who can act to make something happen.

2. Those with agent identities also have the ability walk through their life with certain privileges not available to those living with target identities.

Race privilege is often misunderstood and for many the term "white privilege" creates discomfort and motivates an immediate need to defend their life experiences as no different from people of color.

1. "I've worked hard to get what I have."

2. "My parents sacrificed much so I could go to this university."

3. "My life has not been easy."

I hear these are comments frequently in my work and it is important to note that when talking about your privileges as a white person, it doesn't mean you have not had challenges, difficulties or hardships—*it just means your race was not the cause of those problems.*

We will take a closer look at privilege in Chapter four, but before we do let's take some time here to more closely examine white supremacy which is built on the concept of privilege.

Yes, we need to talk a bit more specifically about white supremacy because many people think it is an identity. Certainly, the images of white men and women and even children waving confederate flags and Nazi symbols armed as if they are getting ready to go to war create a sense of identity—"those people with those beliefs." But white supremacy it not just an identity where a certain group of people communicate or dress in a certain way—white supremacy is an ideology—it is a belief, and it is a way of life based on that belief.

What that means is that white supremacy is a belief system and way of living that has been constructed, communicated, and supported for centuries in the United States and even longer across the globe. Put simply *white supremacy is the belief that white racial identity—and all that comes with it—is better, period. It is superior to all other racial identities and has the right to obtain and remain in positions of power and privilege that control what happens to those living with those other racial identities.* This power has been communicated by:

1. Taking land from Indigenous people in the Americas and failing to follow through on agreements made about land use.

2. Writing "history" and constructing narratives that omitted the reality of the experiences of people of color.

3. Dehumanizing Africans during enslavement across the

world and in the United States—and this included abduction, murder, separating families, criminalizing the behavior of Black men and creating images of them as violent, animalistic brutes; using Black women as "breeders" to increase product and profit.

There are far too many examples to share here, and we will revisit this more in Chapter four with a very vivid example but first a definition of white supremacy from Layla Saad, the author of *Me and White Supremacy: Combat Racism, Change the World and Become a Good Ancestor*: "[T]he idea that white equals better, superior, more worthy, more credible, more deserving, and more valuable from" (Saad 2020).

And how, you ask, did this happen? How did we get here with white supremacy as the norm?

Many find this surprising but white supremacy was normalized in the United States from the founding of the country—but in the following text of a Supreme Court ruling you can see how white supremacy became not just an identity, but an ideology, a belief system that determined how Blacks would be treated in the United States.

"The Black man has no rights which the White man is bound to respect…he may justly and lawfully be reduced to slavery…and treated like an ordinary article of traffic and merchandise."

This is actual wording from U.S. Supreme Court Justice Roger B. Taney in the *Dred Scott vs Sandford* ruling handed down in 1856. In this trial, a formerly enslaved Black man, Dred Scott sued for his freedom because he had been living as a free Black man but when was taken to a state where slavery was still legal, he lost all rights as a free man and was enslaved. This Supreme Court ruling literally legalized white supremacy and anti-Blackness, and the dehumanization of Black people who were declared merchandise, property, and product for profit.

Please sit with that for a moment.

Certainly, outwardly racist systems of oppression like chattel slavery, apartheid, and racial discrimination in employment have been made illegal—so many believe white supremacy is not common. But look at what white supremacy looks like today. This image is an adaptation of both the white supremacy pyramid and the cultural iceberg (links to both are in the resource section.) As you can see in the image there are

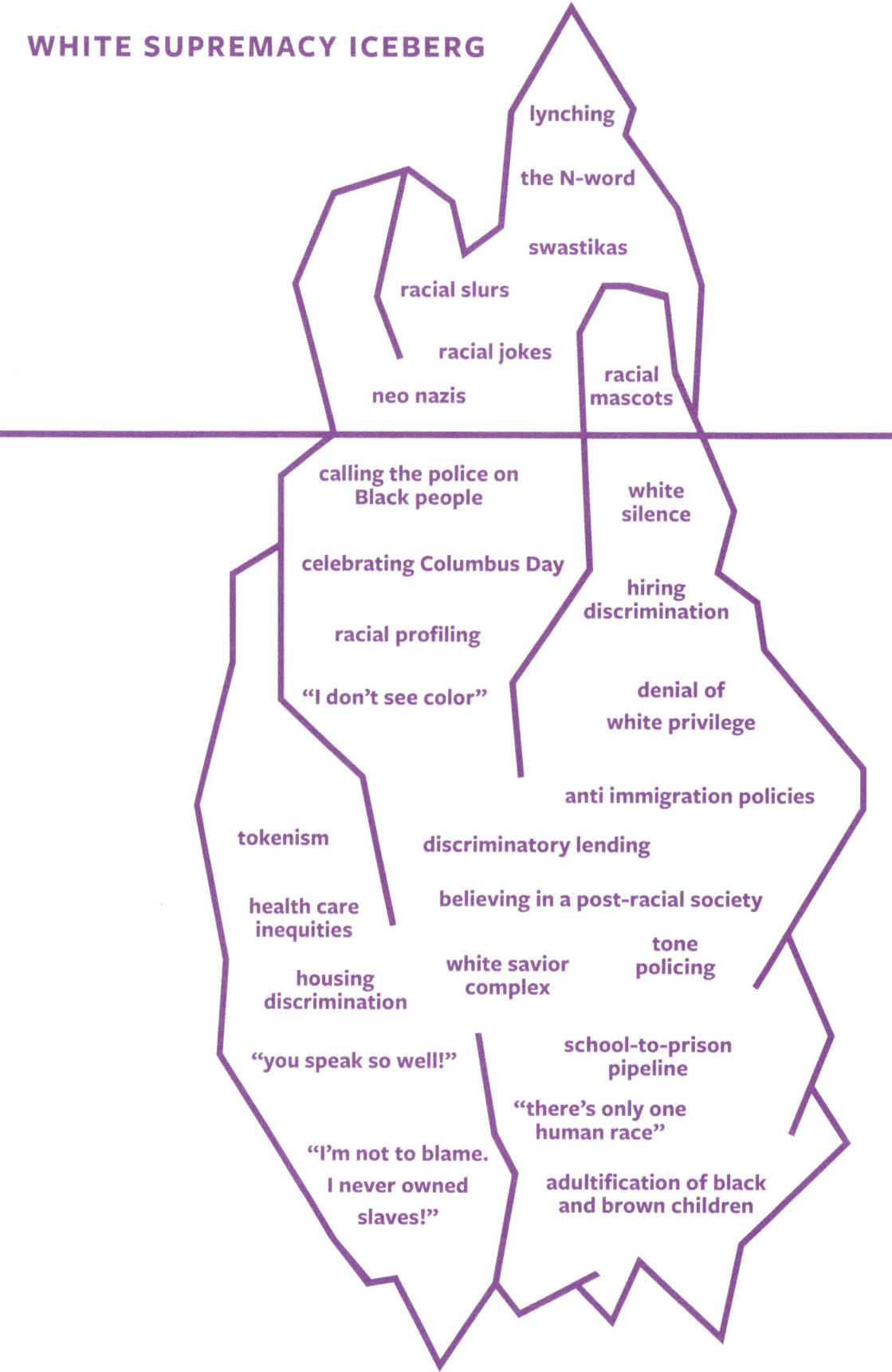

examples of both overt and covert white supremacist actions. Overt white supremacy can be seen, is easily recognized and like the tip of an iceberg can be navigated to avoid danger as such actions are socially unacceptable. Covert white supremacy is not as easily recognized so it is readily accepted but again, like the iceberg what is below the surface can cause significant harm.

White supremacy exists because that particular racial identity as white comes with privileges. No matter how poor a white person may be, or how difficult life may be for them, they learn early in life because of their identity as a white person, they are still better than a person who is not white. And because of that belief that white is inherently better, there is white privilege. Let's take a closer look at privilege to help you better understand what it looks like in everyday life and think more about your own identity privileges.

PRIVILEGE ACTIVITY

I have found that quite often people respond to the term privilege by saying, "my life has been difficult" or "my parents and grandparents worked hard for our family to get where we are." Privilege does not mean you have had a life of ease, without any difficulties or pain—when discussing race privilege for example it means that race was not the cause of those difficulties or pain.

To create a better understanding of privilege here is a reflection activity you can do alone or with another or others on this journey with you. This written version is adapted from the Privilege Walk and the Privilege Beads activities—both are experiential activities often used in social justice education classes. In the resources section are links to those versions if you are interested in learning more about them or how to facilitate them in a group.

To illustrate how identity privilege operates in everyday lived experiences, please take time to do the following activity. Read through each category of identity listed below.

FOR EACH STATEMENT THAT APPLIES TO YOU INDICATE YES WITH A CHECKMARK, OR WRITE "YES" OR "TRUE."

This activity will give you a visual of the privileges you live with because of your identities. Put a check mark next to those statements that apply to you; those that you answer yes to.

Nationality Privilege (think about living in the United States)
- _____ Most people I meet assume that I can speak English.
- _____ I have never been told not to speak in my native language during everyday interactions.
- _____ People do not assume I am poor because of the nation I come from.
- _____ I see people from my nation/country positively represented in politics, business, and the media.
- _____ If I wanted to, and had the resources, I could travel freely to almost any other country.

Sexuality/Sexual Orientation Privilege
- _____ I am able to formalize my love relationship legally through marriage and receive the benefits that come with a legal marriage.
- _____ When I move about in public, I am not afraid of being harassed or physically attacked because of my sexual orientation.
- _____ If my family or friends find out about my sexual orientation, I do not fear there will be consequences—economic, emotional, physical, or psychological.
- _____ No one has ever asked me why I "chose" my sexual orientation.
- _____ I have lived for months, even years, without me or anyone else referring explicitly to my sexuality.

Religious Privilege
- _____ I assume that I will not have to work or go to school on my religious holidays.
- _____ I can find food that is part of my religious practice easily in restaurants or grocery stores.
- _____ My community has numerous places where I can worship or practice.

_____ When those where I work or go to school with refer to or talk about religion it conforms to my own religious beliefs.
_____ When I disclose my religious identity to others I don't worry about problems resulting from that.

Class Privilege

_____ When I need medical or legal help I am sure that my social class will be an advantage.
_____ I am usually sure that I or my family will not have to skip meals because we cannot afford to eat.
_____ I have at least a month's rent, money for food, and other bills, set aside in a savings account in case of emergency.
_____ I vacationed outside of my home country within the past three years.
_____ I have never been unhoused or legally evicted from my place of living.

Race Privilege

_____ When I go shopping I never worry that I will be followed or closely watched by store employees because of my race.
_____ I cannot recall being asked if I got into my college of choice or was hired for a job only because of my race.
_____ If I do well in a challenging situation I won't be called a credit to my race.
_____ I cannot recall being asked to speak for all the people of my race.
_____ It is possible for me to consider many options—social, political, or professional—without asking whether a person of my race would be accepted or allowed to do what I want to do.

Ability Privilege

_____ I assume that I can easily physically access any building.
_____ I have never been taunted, teased, or socially ostracized due to a disability.
_____ I can do well in a challenging situation and not be told what an inspiration I must be to other people of my ability status.
_____ It is easy for me to see and read the letters on this page.
_____ I don't worry that others think that my intelligence is lacking, just because of my physical status or learning difference.

Gender/Sex Privilege

_____ Few people will ask me how I balance my professional and private lives if I have children and a successful career.

_____ It is very likely that I will meet with a person of my gender when I ask to see "the person in charge," and more likely, the higher they are up in the organization, the surer of that I can be.

_____ The majority of sexual objects portrayed in the media are not the same gender as I am.

_____ I don't feel pressure to be thin or to worry about how people will respond to me if I'm overweight.

_____ Leaders in major religions in the world are mainly people of my gender.

Cis Gender Privilege

_____ When I use public restrooms I don't fear verbal abuse, physical intimidation, or arrest.

_____ As I move through the world, I am not being constantly stared or gawked at, whispered about, pointed at, or laughed at because of the way I express my gender.

_____ Gender exclusive spaces such as women's centers, womyn's music festivals, and gendered athletic teams will not exclude me because of my trans status.

_____ I can flirt or date and not fear that my biological status may be the cause for rejection or attack.

_____ My ability to acquire a job, rent an apartment, or secure a loan will not be denied because of my gender identity/expression.

REFLECTING ON YOUR PRIVILEGES

When you have completed this activity take some time to reflect on it and respond to prompts below.

1. What was your initial reaction to this activity? How did it make you feel? What were your thoughts as you were completing it?

   _____
   _____
   _____
   _____
   _____

2. Which category of privilege has the most marks for yes?
   _____
   _____

3. What surprised you about the number of privileges you have—or do not have?
   _____
   _____
   _____
   _____
   _____
   _____

4. Who do you know who would have different responses to the questions in a specific category?
   _____
   _____
   _____
   _____

5. When have there been opportunities for them to share that reality with you?
   _____
   _____
   _____
   _____
   _____
   _____

How does this activity create more awareness of communication across identity differences and racial divisions in:

your everyday interactions?
   _____
   _____
   _____
   _____
   _____

the larger cultural contexts of your family, profession, community, country or even globally?

_____
_____
_____
_____
_____

6. How can you use your privilege in those communication contexts to interrupt, intervene and inform others about the beliefs, ideas and actions that create and sustain identity divisions—and dehumanization?

_____
_____
_____
_____
_____
_____
_____
_____
_____
_____

As you reflect on this activity and your responses to the questions think about how your commitment to learn more, do different and move forward to transform yourself and society can include using your privileges—that is also what you can bring to communicative contexts about racial differences and identity divisions.

A thought before moving on...
As we end this exploration of what you bring to communication about race, across identity differences and divisions, I want to leave you with a few thoughts that are important before we take a larger look at communication in cultural contexts that supported social injustice, discrimination, dehumanization, and anti-Blackness. I think it is important to first understand that your own communication can support and further racial divisions—and this is not to make you feel ashamed or guilty but

to help you to understand how changing your own communication can help support change in larger society…and not just your words, hashtags, or memes, but in your everyday actions and interactions.

But once more, I want to be clear and brutally honest here about what I know for sure: Communication across difference, across social identities and racial divisions to "dialogue for better understanding" is a process. And recall what I have said previously:

It is not easy.

There are no *hacks*.

With this review of the communication process, I hope you see that the only aspect of the process you can really control is what you bring to the interaction—so sit with that. Yes, you are culpable, **but also know you are empowered as well to change what you do as an individual and that is what is needed to transform the larger society.**

But this requires courage…as you think about what you can do as an individual work through the following activity and keep it close by. After you read the next chapter where we will explore the larger backstory of racial identity and specifically anti-Blackness, you may want to revisit the activity to further sustain your courage on the path.

REFLECTION

I offer you the following to consider alone or even with another or with others in a group:

What actions can help you learn more about your stuff and how to "unpack" it so you can participate in transforming society.

How are you going to access the information you believe you need to educate yourself?

What can you read?

Who can you talk to?

How can you improve your own communication across and about identity differences and racial divisions?

CHAPTER FOUR

COMMUNICATING ANTI-BLACKNESS IN THE BACKSTORY: DISMANTLING TAKES COURAGE

IN CHAPTERS ONE through three we examined the process of communication, identity socialization, and what you bring with identity in your interactions, including race privilege and an ideology of white supremacy. I hope it also helped you to better understand how that identity as part of your stuff impacts your communication about race and across identity divisions. This is your backstory and your honest exploration requires curiosity and courage; (two of the Four "Cs") and I hope you will keep both close by in this chapter where the focus is on the backstory of race and anti-Blackness in the United States. (And again, while I use my own country for our exploration of white supremacy and anti-Blackness in the Primer, I emphasize these concepts are experienced across the world, every day). As you read in the previous chapter, white supremacy in the United States (and globally) was legalized and the effects continue to impact the everyday lived experiences of millions of people who are still not treated as fully human because of their racial identity—in fact, they are dehumanized.

This chapter examines the backstory of race in the United States and also provides discussions and explanations to help you better understand words and terms you hear when talking about social injustice, anti-Black racism, resisting racism, and dismantling systems of oppression and dehumanization. This will help you to become more informed as you talk about the legacy of social injustice, privilege and power and better understand how those concepts are communicated and supported in interpersonal interactions and in public policy. It will clarify the use of "systemic" when referring to communication in relationships that may crystallize into rigid structures that are difficult to change or tear apart. It doesn't mean putting the blame on one person or individual as the origin of social injustice and anti-Black racism—though there can be individuals participating in situations that support and perpetuate the system. In this chapter we will also discuss Critical Race Theory, social in/justice language, and explanations of terms you may encounter as you read more to learn more and do different.

WARNING:

Yes, you read that right, this Primer contains a discussion of **Critical Race Theory!**

As I worked on this Primer during the summer of 2021, I could not help but notice that the backlash against Critical Race Theory (CRT) in education, government and even individual communities grew louder as many whites in the country encountered information they say is a "rewriting of U.S. history" intended to make them feel guilty and ashamed. That is not what Critical Race Theory is and this is a great place for me to offer you a response you can share if you encounter such backlash. It is also a good place to start a chapter that talks about Critical Race Theory.

There are many places where you can find not just definitions but scholarly articles and books about Critical Race Theory. But again, as this is a Primer, I want to keep it simple to help you better understand it and motivate you to learn more. In all honesty, this Primer is an example of Critical Race Theory, which is an academic concept explaining the way things are (as do most theories). Critical Race Theory says, race is not biology—but rather it is socially constructed, built on ways of thinking and communicating that support beliefs about those living with certain racial identities. In other words, meaning is given to those racial identities and it is the act of giving meaning that creates and constructs the difference, divisions and dehumanization. In addition, the backstory of race in the United States, and globally, is a narrative or a story of how white racial identity is better (supremacy) and where people of color are perceived as less than and inferior, dismissed, devalued and dehumanized. In the story, they are the "others" who are "othered" through messages continuously communicated to and about them every day, all day in their lives. As a result of that story being told for centuries, people believe, embrace, and pass it on so that human interaction in everyday lived experiences across centuries of cultural contexts, communicate the belief that Blacks, for example, are dangerous, inferior, less intelligent, and criminals deserving of punishment or death even when they are not threatening to harm anyone.

Critical Race Theory began with legal scholars who also challenged the belief that *"that there is only one way to be Black"* as if your other social identities do not influence your life and realities in everyday human interactions. Other social identities such as gender, social economic class, and religion intersect with racial identity and influence lived experiences of one who identifies as Black. Critical Race Theory reinforces what most people of color know: racism in the United States is an ordinary experience for them with stereotypes of their race informing all forms of interaction with whites who bring their stuff. Think again about Emily and LaKisha applying for the same job. Even though legal action and the creation of the mid-twentieth century Equal Employment Opportunity Commission prohibited race from being used as a reason not to hire someone, it is still being used in the twenty-first century thanks to implicit bias. Critical Race Theory helps explain and affirm why this continues—it is part of the larger backstory of U.S. race and racism that today justifies why unarmed Black men, women and children can be killed without legal consequences for those who killed them.

Admittedly this is a simple description but as a place to begin you can see how this Primer offers a start to a long journey of unlearning and relearning what many white people want to make illegal—the truth is often hard to hear. And some white people believe it puts their race privilege at risk. I also think the truth telling of race in the U.S creates a particular kind of fear. Think of it this way: *"The people who threw rocks at young Black children as they walked into segregated schools for the first time don't want their grandchildren to know they threw rocks at, and spit on, these children just for wanting to go to school"*

Sit with that a moment. Then consider how hard it might be for many white people to respond to their children's or grandchildren's questions about why they believe some races are inferior and should be treated as less than or even deserve violence. How do they explain Jim Crow laws and images of vicious German shepherd dogs brutally attacking young Black men and women peacefully protesting in Civil

Rights movement marches while police sprayed them with high powered water hoses and beat them? This is why here, in the third decade of the twenty-first century, a movement to make teaching Critical Race Theory illegal and the banning of books emerged with such fury—if you don't know how to talk about race and the racial past, it is easier to ignore it. Opponents of CRT say they don't want their children to read books that will make them feel ashamed for being white because of what happened *in the past*, but it is probably also true that they don't want to have to answer questions about their own participation in, or support of, racial discrimination *now*. Is there a way to not only learn more about the historical backstory to do different when interacting across and about racial identity differences and divisions, but also learn how to work through fear, guilt and shame and talk about race? That is what this Primer is designed to help you do.

In early summer 2022 it became clear that this fear of talking about the reality of race and identity divisions has motivated and mobilized mass murders of people of color. In May 2022 a gunman entered a Buffalo, New York grocery store and killed 10 people, most of them Black. He had driven 3 hours across the state and visited the store the day before he entered it and began firing an assault weapon. His social media manifesto referred to "replacement theory" or the belief that many white nationalists claim is designed to change the racial demographics of the United States and future elections. This chapter is an appropriate place to examine an unfounded theory that illustrates the deep fear of communicating honestly about racism, anti-Blackness, and dehumanization in order to begin the process of affirming the humanity of all identities.

This theory is not new. It has always been part of the backstory of race in the United States but rapid communication in digital technology now make it more accessible for those who want to embrace the ideology. But what is also true is that there are, again, voices, actions and movements fueled by those who are committed to dismantling dehumanization and systemic oppression. Later in this chapter are explanations of words and terms you may find useful to support your commitment to better communication across differences and divisions.

Replacement theory states that the Jewish community is responsible for leading the replacement of white people with people of color; those living with identities that have historically been treated as inferior, less than and dehumanized. This theory is easily seen in the actions of those embracing movements that are obviously fear fueled calls for a return to the original racial and religious foundation of the United States of America. Those who speak about and spread replacement theory, those who support it, and those who enact violence in the name of stopping the "replacement," are afraid of a growing diverse population in the United States—a country founded on the principle that "All men are created equal"—a declaration that has never been the lived reality in this country, has it? Let's start by acknowledging that those who wrote those words, were white, wealthy, landowning men and that is also who they envisioned when they wrote those words. Since the founding of this country, look at what has been done historically to deny the *equality of all humans* and repeatedly keep the country "great" for whites:

1. Manifest Destiny, a phrase coined in 1845, is the idea that the United States is destined—by God, its advocates believed—to expand its dominion and spread democracy and capitalism across the entire North American continent. This led to the genocide, slaughter and removal of the indigenous Native American people who were already living on land "discovered" by Europeans.

2. The enslavement of Africans brought humans to the United States as products to build a country and further capitalism while denying their existence as human beings. Enslavement was ended only after the Civil War divided the country into those who wanted to keep the dehumanization of human beings legal—and those who did not.

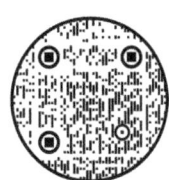

3. The Chinese Exclusion Act passed in 1882 prohibited Chinese laborers from entering the United States. The Act was a result of anti-Chinese movements in California and throughout the west coast. In the late nineteenth century, the Chinese constituted a large racial minority and found success working in the growing mining industry. After developing skills for finding gold, resentment developed, and the Chinese were excluded from the mining industry and moved to more urban areas where they were allowed to work only in specific occupations.

4. Japanese internment camps were created in 1942 by President Franklin D. Roosevelt after the bombing of Pearl Harbor fueled fears of further violence and espionage. As a result, 120,000 Americans of Japanese descent were forcibly removed from their homes—the majority of whom were American citizens. Called relocation centers, the prison camps were located across the U.S. and closed in 1946. Many of those imprisoned lost their homes, businesses, and property that was never returned to them. In 1988, Congress offered an apology to Japanese Americans and twenty thousand dollars in reparations to those affected.

5. Jim Crow laws in the United States further legalized the dehumanization of Blacks in the country for almost a century after enslavement ended. The laws were a way of life in mainly U.S. southern states but also operated in northern areas of the country. Jim Crow legalized the treatment of Blacks as second-class citizens with laws determining where you could go to school, shop, eat, live, or walk on a sidewalk. Breaking the law—even ones that prohibited a Black person from entering through a front door of a business—could get a Black person killed—and that killing was legal. Jim Crow was justified by people in positions of power by spreading the belief Blacks were inferior, less than human and further legitimized the belief that whites were better, a white supremacist ideology that still exists today in the U.S.

With your commitment to learn more and do different and dismantle racism, anti-Blackness and the belief that the white race is the only right race and superior, we must ask when was America great? And for whom? And by the way, America is the continent on which the United States is located America is not a country. The United States is the country that needs to be "saved" from the blatant hate and dehumanization that has been the reality and its legacy.

Replacement theory is being spread by those in political power and on televised and social media spaces who know the fear is real for

This 1870s engraving depicts an enslaved woman and young girl being auctioned as property.
Universal History Archive/Universal Images Group/Getty Images

white people who see a changing demographic that includes far more voices demanding all identities be treated as humans. These are voices that were once slaughtered, enslaved, systemically denied access to the "American dream," and, yes, still today dehumanized—but they can no longer be silenced. Hearing these voices creates fear in whites who believe in replacement theory. The fear is that if people of color are humanized and treated as truly equal, with equity in all areas of their life, white people will lose something—right? That fear is the loss of a position of power and privilege that comes with an identity as white; an identity that has allowed whites to treat people of color as less than human while living with the privileges of their own racial identity believed to be not only the best, but believed to be only real race, so unquestionably superior to all the rest.

SOCIAL JUSTICE/INJUSTICE TERMS

In this section I offer brief descriptions of words and terms that are important in communication about racial differences and identity divisions. This brief introduction can help you in conversations and communication as you proceed to learn more to do different.

It is important to note that these are not necessarily definitions, but rather an illustration of some of the ways people, organizations and communities use these terms. What you will read here are composites of definitions found in multiple locations including The Western States Center in Portland, OR.; Program for Intergroups Relations at the University of Michigan; Catalyst.org and a sample of current social justice literature. Do not think of this list as the only interpretation of these words. There are obviously more locations where you can find more definitions and read more about the concepts. This, again, is offered to help as you begin your journey, and the appendix offers additional resources to learn more.

Agent Group: Those who are born with, or acquire, an identity with benefits that grant them privileges over other individuals is a member of an agent group. Agent groups have the power to act and their actions often result in the exploitation of those who have target group identities or identities without power and the ability to act. Instead, they are individuals who are acted on.

Ally: Someone who takes action to support the equal treatment, equity, and affirmation of those with identities who are in underrepresented or marginalized groups.

Anti-racism: This is a noun that describes efforts and activities aimed at identifying and uncovering racism in self, within communities, organizations, and larger society. The goal of anti-racism is to advocate for equity, inclusion, and justice.

Bias: A preference in favor of, or against a person, group of people, or a thing. All humans have bias about something or more accurately, we are biased about many things and our reactions to them are often unconscious. The reactions can be the result of unfounded, inaccurate information and in the case of race and identity differences actions motivated by the bias can harm, prevent the affirmation of humanity of another, and justify dehumanization.

Black Lives Matter (BLM): There are many who still question the need for this phrase and activism related to it. Think of it this way: for more than 400 years, people of African descent, those with an amount of melanin in their skin tone that led them to be identified as Black have been treated as inferior, less than, deficient, deviant and even not fully human, so their lives did not matter. The global slave trade that involved Africans being bought and sold as property meant Black lives only mattered when they resulted in profit for the owner. The dehumanization and devaluation of Black lives continued after enslavement ended. And in the United States the dehumanization and devaluation of Black lives was legalized by Jim Crow laws that prohibited Blacks from living as fully human. The fight for Civil Rights in the mid-twentieth century was a fight for the recognition of Blacks as fully human and in this era some progress was made with policies dismantled and laws passed. The reality, however, is that life as a Black person in the twenty-first century is still filled with barriers to being treated as fully human in both interpersonal interaction and public policy. The police killings of unarmed Black men, women and children became a tipping point and the Black Lives Matter movement brought widespread attention to the painful reality of anti-Blackness. For the BLM movement to happen someone had to first communicate those Black lives do not matter is a reality that occurred for centuries. Racism and anti-Blackness is such a major part of the history of the United States, when you call it out, and try to help people understand what it means, many of them say such that such work is un-American and divisive. Learning about the dehumanization of Black and Indigenous People of Color in the U.S. and working to eliminate it is not un-American as many are claiming, it is honoring and affirming humanity.

Black Indigenous People of Color (BIPOC): The acronym BIPOC, has been used to emphasize the identities of Black and Indigenous as distinct from an identity as a person of color because of the differences in the lived experiences of racism and oppression. In other words, people of color face different forms of injustice than Black and Indigenous people. But this does not mean some injustices are worse than others, all forms of injustice must be dismantled. An example of the need for this distinction is that those of Asian descent are people of color but do not have the same history of oppression as people of African descent in the United States. People of Color (POC) was first used in the 1960s and 70s as a form of protest and solidarity for those rejecting the term "colored people" that was used in the United States to identify someone who was not identified as a white person and was treated as inferior. POC does not refer to a real biological or scientific difference between people but is used to refer to individuals in the United States (and globally) who share the common experience of being targeted and oppressed by racism. Here is a resource for more information on the history of this term.

Colorism or shadism: Another creation of white supremacist ideology is the belief that has white skin is the one true, valued tone and any darker shades, with more melanin are inferior and unattractive. As a result, colorism exists in communities where racial identities include skin tones varying from very light almost white, to very dark. Colorism and shadism support prejudice for lighter skin tones within groups and between-group members—because they are closer to whiteness.

Emotional Tax: The need to always be on guard and protect oneself from the daily harms and dangers of bias, prejudice, individual and systemic oppression is exhausting for people with identities that have been dehumanized. It effects all areas of life, emotional, physical, spiritual, and professional; it takes a toll on well-being and is taxing.

Equality and equity: The belief that treating everyone the same way will affirm the humanity of all identities and support their pursuit of happiness, success and well-being, is equality. The problem, however, is it assumes that all identities have the same opportunities, and the playing field is the same for all. Equity is working to create and support outcomes for people or groups by addressing their unique barriers or advantages.

Ethnicity: A concept often used to identify a group of people who share a particular history, language, geographical region, religion, and/or racial homogeneity who also develop beliefs, behaviors, and traditions that they hold common.

Implicit bias: A negative or positive belief that a person unknowingly holds about other people and is expressed unconsciously. Bias affects attitudes and emotions and results in real actions with real life implications. Everyone has implicit biases about social identities and even though someone may claim to "not see color" or "love everyone" their bias can be revealed in their actions toward those with different identities who are not part of their ingroup.

Individual oppression: Communication between individuals (one-on-one or in small groups) can send messages that discriminate, devalue, and dehumanize someone living with a target group identity. These messages can prevent access to what is needed for well-being, success, and the affirmation of their humanity.

Institutional oppression: Communication in institutions and systems send messages through policies, laws, rules, norms, and customs that are enacted by organizations and social institutions such as religion, government, education, law, the media, and the health care system. The goal of those messages is to disadvantage some social groups and advantage other social groups.

Intersectionality: We all have more than one social identity and they overlap in ways that influence and impact our lived experiences. For those living with multiple identities that have been historically dehumanized the intersections are difficult and dangerous barriers to well-being and success and are a constant reality. Legal scholar Kimberlé Crenshaw coined the term intersectionality to describe a framework for understanding how social identities (such as gender, race, ethnicity, social class, religion, sexual orientation, ability, and gender identity) overlap with one another and with systems of power that oppress and disadvantage people in the workplace and broader community.

Microaggression: Look at this word: micro means small, and aggression is violence, so this means small acts of violence and in our everyday lived experiences it is done through communication. Professor and scholar Derald Wang Sue (2007) defines microaggressions as: "verbal, nonverbal, and environmental slights, snubs, or insults, whether intentional or unintentional, which communicate hostile, derogatory, or negative messages to target persons based solely upon their marginalized group membership."

Oppression: You may hear this term often and it can be either individual, institutional or systemic. To understand how it can exist across contexts consider this definition provided by philosophy scholar Marilyn Frye who says oppression as "the exercise of authority or power in a burdensome, cruel, or unjust manner" (Frye 1989).

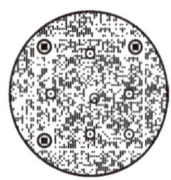

People of Color (POC): was first used in the 1960s and 70s as a form of protest and solidarity for those rejecting the term "colored people" that was used in the United States to identify someone who was not identified as a white person and was treated as inferior. POC does not refer to a real biological or scientific difference between people but is used to refer to individuals in the United States (and globally) who share the common experience of being targeted and oppressed by racism. In the margin is a resource for more information on the history of this term.

Power: The ability to access resources that support and enhance your wellbeing and safety so you can lead a comfortable and productive life. The ability to access resources is more readily available to individuals living with identities from agent groups where power is one of many unearned benefits of that identity.

Privilege: Many social identities have benefits and advantages individuals enjoy simply because they are member of an agent group. Privilege is not a matter of what you have been given to support you in life but rather the absence of obstacles such as discrimination and systemic oppression that you don't have to navigate in your everyday lived experiences. For example, race privilege doesn't mean you have not had difficulties in life, it means that race was not the reason for the barriers you had to overcome.

Race: This is not based on biology—it is a social construct that artificially divides individuals into distinct groups based on characteristics such as the amount of melanin in skin, ancestry, cultural history and/or ethnicity. But even though race is not real the experiences of living with a racial identity are real and hard to avoid.

Racism: Thoughts and actions that reflect prejudice and discrimination based on differences in racial and ethnic identities. Historically and currently these beliefs were enacted against persons of color by white/European descent groups with power to support their actions.

Racism is racial prejudice plus power, and it is used to exploit and dehumanize persons of color based on a belief in the superiority of the white race and the privileges of that identity.

Racial justice: The systemic equitable treatment of people of all races across all contexts of interpersonal and societal interaction resulting in opportunities for wellbeing, and liberty safety for all.

Salient: When an individual is conscious of their social identity and the implications of it in everyday lived experiences it becomes an important part of life, often hard to ignore. It affects them emotionally and physically because they recognize prominence and the problems they face because of that identity.

Social identity: Refers to an aspect of identity that develops in relation to others in everyday lived experiences and is defined by race, gender, class, sexual orientation, social class, religion, ability and age. Membership in one of the agent identity groups often offers access to power and privilege that those in target identity groups do not experience.

Structural racism: When institutions such as the government, education, health care, legal system, and corporate organizations explicitly or implicitly provide unfair advantages that allow access and success of some individuals over others based on their race.

Systemic oppression: Similar to institutional oppression, communication in systems send messages through policies, laws, rules, norms, and customs that are enacted by organizations and social institutions such as religion, government, education, law, the media, and health care system. The goal of those messages sent repeatedly, across contexts are to disadvantage some social groups and advantage other social groups.

Target group: Target groups are made up of those with identities who do not have power and ability to act, they are individuals who are acted on by those in agent groups. This happens in many ways such as disenfranchisement, exploitation, and victimization in ways that prevent accessing resources needed to support well-being and safety.

White supremacy: Layla Saad (2020) offers this concise but thorough definition: "The historic and modern legislating, societal conditioning, and systemic institutionalizing of the construction of whiteness as inherently superior to people of other races."

"Othering"

To this list of terms, I now add one of my own to help us in this chapter—"othering." What do I mean by othering?

Othering happens when someone with an identity different than yours is seen as not just different, but somehow less than, inferior, or perhaps only a stereotype—an inaccurate representation sustained by a lack of real interaction with the person or members of that person's social group. Even worse, one who is "different," "them," or "those people," can be seen and interacted with not as fully human but as an imagined being based on what you have been told, taught and now believe.

Think about examples of "othering" you have seen.

How might you communicate in ways that "other"?

Take a moment to reflect.

Fill in the blank with a belief you may have about the "other" that is not a result of human interaction but media representations, or what you were told about "those people." Acting on those beliefs creates distance, devalues their lived experiences, and even dehumanizes them.

They/those people are: _____
_____
_____

"Othering" is based on a biased belief about "them" that you embraced at some point in your socialization. Using the terms "those people" and "them" create divisions and those words imply "they" are not like us—and this is especially important when actions follow those words and beliefs about "those people."

Now take a moment and revisit your Backstory Bag©—what and where did you learn about certain racial groups—more specifically groups unlike your own?

Othering is often justified because it is common—but that is exactly the challenge—that is what is meant by dismantling systems of oppression. Recall our definition of oppression: *The exercise of authority or power in a burdensome, cruel, or unjust manner.* Philosophy scholar Marilyn Frye compared oppression to a bird cage noting in her 1989 journal article: "any given wire of the cage may or may not be specifically developed for the purpose of trapping the bird, yet it still operates (together with the other wires) to restrict its freedom" (Frye, 1989).

This is the reality, the lived experience of many who are disenfranchised and marginalized by identity, the cage restricts and confines, so they are locked out—*or in* by a system of interlocking oppressions and race is a primary one. When activists talk about "dismantling systems of oppression and racism" it is a call to undo, do different, to stop believing that Black, Brown and Indigenous people in the United States are inferior, deficient, deviant, and dangerous and to eliminate the personal actions and public policies that built those beliefs and have supported their existence for centuries.

The U.S. history of othering people of African descent began with enslavement but continued well after emancipation, throughout the twentieth century and is still evident today. It continues because it operates through the power dynamics of target and agent identities discussed in chapter three and in the terms in the previous section—recall:

1. Target groups are those living with social identities that are disenfranchised and exploited. Targets are acted on.

2. Agent groups are those living with unearned privileges and are in positions of power. Agents do the acting.

This dynamic results in systems of authority that can be exercised in a burdensome, cruel, or unjust manner. In that system who gets to "other," what does othering look like, and how did it begin?

African enslavement: Dehumanization for product and profit...*to build a country*

Systemic racism and anti-Blackness began and was firmly established when enslaved Africans were brought to the United States as products for profit—not human beings. They were products necessary to participate in a capitalist enterprise—yes to make money. Human beings were seen as products, and property needed to produce profit. Period.

In Chapter three I mentioned Dred Scott, an enslaved Black man who sued for his freedom and lost. In April 1846, Dred and his wife Harriet filed for freedom in the St. Louis Circuit Court based on two Missouri statutes. One allowed any person of any color to sue for wrongful enslavement and the other stated that any person taken to a free territory automatically became a free person and therefore could not be re-enslaved upon returning to a slave state.

The case made its way through the state levels of arguments and rulings with Scott appealing it to the U.S. Supreme Court where an 1857 ruling justified the dehumanization of Blacks and condoned their use as property. Below, is text from that ruling.

The Black man has no rights which the White man is bound to respect...He may justly and lawfully be reduced to slavery... and treated as an ordinary article of traffic and merchandise.

U.S. Supreme Court Chief Justice Roger B. Taney, Dred Scott v. Sandford

Read the New York Times The 1619 Project for an excellent review of the African slave trade, consequences, and implications for the lived experiences of Black people—and not just then but also now. You can find out more about it in the resource section.

It is easy to see in these words a declaration and confirmation of white supremacy. And this is an example of cultural context—yes, in the cultural context of enslavement, Africans arriving in the U.S. were not seen as human—but product and property for profit.

Many people like to believe after legalized slavery ended in 1865 this ideology ended also but we know that is not true as the Jim Crow era in the twentieth century in the U.S. proves. Recall Rosa Parks was arrested when she refused to move to the back of the bus where Blacks—or "Coloreds" as we were called then—were supposed to sit when whites boarded and wanted a seat in the front. Here again is that power and privilege we talked about. Historic images of the Jim Crow policies in the southern United States include separate water fountains and public restrooms or whites and "Coloreds."

If you haven't seen the movie *Hidden Figures*—the story of how Black women played a critical role at NASA, the National Aeronautics and Space Administration in the United States' mid-twentieth century race to space—you should for many reasons and to see a very explicit example of the implications of different bathrooms. Although the filmmakers admit this was not an actual event from the life of the character Katherine Johnson it does provide a compelling and troubling look at the reality of that time. And the fact that the story of these amazing woman was not told until the early twenty-first century is again another example of the history of devaluing Black people and diminishing their amazing contributions—done by whites in positions of power that supported excluding Blacks' significance and success.

A GANG OF FEMALE SLAVES—CENTRAL AFRICA.

A few of the Jim Crow policies communicating inferiority and dehumanization included:

1. Dining for Blacks often meant going to the restaurant backdoor for food to be eaten elsewhere and not being seated in the restaurant—it wasn't called carryout then.

2. At movie theaters Black people were allowed to sit in the balcony only—when they were allowed entry.

3. Blacks had to move off the sidewalk if they were in the pathway of an oncoming white person—refusal to do so came with consequences.

And because these were policies and laws, violation meant severe punishment, including death with little chance of a white assailant being charged for it. The belief in white supremacy justified killing a Black

person who broke the law—even when that law was dehumanizing and unjust.

The Jim Crow Museum at Ferris State University provides a painful look at Jim Crow policies and practices that communicated the inferiority of Blacks in the U.S. and maintained segregation and dehumanization. The website is excellent resource to learn more about the backstory of U.S. race and racism. Scan the code here to access the museum website and learn more about the origin of the term Jim Crow.

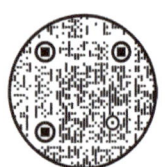

Throughout the 1830s and '40s, the white entertainer Thomas Dartmouth Rice (1808-1860) performed a popular song-and-dance act supposedly modeled after a slave. He named the character Jim Crow. Rice darkened his face, acted like a buffoon, and spoke with an exaggerated and distorted imitation of African American Vernacular English. In his Jim Crow persona, he also sang "Negro ditties" such as "Jump Jim Crow." Rice was not the first white comic to perform in Blackface, but he was the most popular of his time, touring both the United States and England. As a result of Rice's success, "Jim Crow" became a common stage persona for white comedians' Blackface portrayals of African Americans. After the American Civil War (1861-1865), most southern states and, later, border states passed laws that denied Blacks basic human rights. It is not clear how, but the minstrel character's name "Jim Crow" became a kind of shorthand for the laws, customs and etiquette that segregated and demeaned African Americans primarily from the 1870s to the 1960s.

The website also includes a list of Jim Crow laws and images such as the ones on this page.

While the segregation policies of the southern United States were more visible and blatant, that does not mean the Jim Crow attitudes and ideology was not in the north. It was indeed.

One example I recall from childhood summer family road trips to take my older brother and cousins (the garage band group I wanted to

join as a drummer) to Boy Scout camps in all-white southern Illinois communities that were "sundown towns." These signs gave warnings to Blacks passing through with very explicit roadside signs with warnings such as: "Niggers don't let the sun set on you here." While my parents, aunts, and uncles never spoke specifically about the danger, they often spoke in quick, clipped phrases about "these places" as we passed by miles of cows and corn and their hushed tones fueled my curiosity. And yes, they always made sure when the sun was beginning to set, we were close to our all-Black hometown of East St. Louis.

REDLINING

A very vivid and painful example of white supremacy, power, and privilege functioning as a system to not just exclude but dehumanize Blacks in the U.S. is **redlining**.

Redlining is a discriminatory lending practice where the lender denies a mortgage loan because of the race of the applicant and prevents them from moving into white neighborhoods. The term *redlining* came about in reference to the use of red marks on maps that loan corporations would use to outline mixed-race or Black neighborhoods. Neighborhoods in more-affluent areas, which were deemed most worthy of loans, were usually outlined in blue or green. Neighborhoods outlined in yellow were also considered desirable for lending.

In the 1930s, the U.S. federal government created programs to encourage homeownership and the development of the suburbs with affordable mortgages. But neighborhoods with primarily Black residents were considered high risk and excluded—and the policies created housing segregation still exist. To support segregation many white neighborhoods enacted racial covenants—an actual statement in the home deed that prohibited the sale of the home to a Black person or person of color.

After World War II, housing segregation was further supported when white soldiers were given approval for VA loans for homes in suburbs while Blacks were denied. This is how the suburbs became white. And yes, you read that right, the United States government supported racial segregation in housing. Here is a very real, very vivid and painful example of target identities acted on by agent identities—and in this case the agent is the federal government.

After the federal Fair Housing Act was passed in 1968, Blacks did start moving into predominantly white neighborhoods and whites—acting on their beliefs that Blacks were less human, inferior, and dangerous, fled. This is known as white flight and happened initially when whites left urban areas for the suburbs after WWII and repeated it again in the 1970s and 80s when Blacks began moving into previously segregated white suburbs. The consequences of white flight fueled by an ideology of othering and fear of "those people" had major consequences for predominantly Black neighborhoods in both urban and suburban communities:

- White flight began because Blacks moved in.
- Whites sold houses cheap to get away from "them" quickly.
- Businesses left not wanting to interact with, or sell to, "them."
- Taxes generated in the community dropped significantly.

One grave consequence of low/little tax base: less money for education and students are the ones who suffer because of the lack of resources.

I choose education as an example because it helps to reveal much about race, privilege, power, white supremacy and a deliberate, systemic, century of dehumanization that continues to be communicated in both personal actions and public policy. Here is a closer look:

We all know that we are told good school systems cost money and locations with a healthy tax base can support a good school system. It is no secret that parents will often look for a home in an area with good schools so they can give their children the benefit of a good education that will grant them access and availability to pursue and participate in the American Dream where success includes a life of liberty and justice.

An example of the flip side of that ideology is the belief that without a good education or with a substandard high school education one:

- cannot get into "good" colleges.
- cannot get "good" jobs.
- cannot make "good" money.
- cannot pursue dreams of happiness.
- cannot reap the benefits of home ownership.

In this example we can see how even as an adult it is still hard to "act" as agent when you live with an identity that has been historically "targeted" to be devalued and dehumanized and excluded from pursuing the success of the American Dream. The government participation in housing segregation in the U.S. is a clear example of systemic racism and how target identities are *acted on*—and controlled by those in power.

Oh, yes, and let us not forget that historically equity in one's home served as a resource that enabled contributions to children's college funds, startup funds for a business, purchase for a better home in a better neighborhood, or inheritance. With decades of exclusion from homeownership Black Americans remain far behind in such goals. But this is not to say all Blacks have no equity in their homes, many do and as we know many have pursued and participated in the American Dream—while still fighting for that "liberty and justice *for all*." However, this discussion of housing segregation does demonstrate how a system has created notable and significant differences across race and wealth resulting in inequalities known as disparities.

While we would like to believe otherwise, the practice of redlining continues and the effects of it live on. One very vivid and painful reality are food deserts in many urban areas. A food desert is an area in a city or community that has few, if any, options for residents to buy food that supports good health.

Food deserts are the result of decades of white flight, leaving little to no tax support from businesses who are unwilling to operate in areas with "those people." And please remember that long-term, the inability

to eat healthy food, and relying only on fast food or prepacked, highly processed food sold in convenience stores can result in long-term chronic health problems such as diabetes, heart disease, and high blood pressure. These are chronic health conditions diagnosed in Black people more often—also called health disparities. This an example of the consequence of the twentieth century redlining that destroyed urban neighborhoods where many Black families were forced to remain when they could not obtain houses in the suburbs. It is also an example of systemic racism.

If you have not heard about redlining, how the government created housing segregation and the consequences of it—you are not alone. I've found that many if not most of the whites in the U.S. don't know about redlining because they don't have to know about it because of their race privilege. Redlining is what it looks like when race privilege, power, policies—and even policing work together in a system of racist interpersonal actions supported by public policies and actions that enforce them.

With this discussion it becomes clearer how agent identities are privileged.

1. They have the ability to act rather than get acted on.
2. They are not attacked.
3. They are not ridiculed.
4. They are not affected by action or development.

WHY NOT? *Because*

1. They exert power.
2. They make the decisions.
3. They create the effects—that benefit them.

And that is privilege. It is often said that privilege is when you think something is not a problem because it is not a problem to you personally.

Conclusion For Part One: Reflecting to Move Forward

As we conclude this chapter and the first part of the Primer, my hope is that you have discovered information that might help you answer the question that motivates many to engage in anti-racist work and seek out sources for social justice education: How did we get here? We know the answer is a combination of personal and social backstory; it is the stuff we bring to communication across so many contexts. This insight can be empowering and if you are wondering what you can do to do different, know that awareness is the first step and there are specific communication skills you can learn to develop the ability and build your capacity to talk about race and across identity divisions.

The first part of this Primer offered insight into the process of human communication, a better understanding of your own backstory and the backstory of race and racism, privilege and power, and the implications of racial identities, anti-Blackness, and systemic racism in that process of human interaction.

If you are uncomfortable or angry about what you've learned, feel guilty or ashamed that you did not know more about race and identity in your own backstory and the backstory of race in the U.S. I hope you are now thinking about how you can learn more to do different in your interaction and communication and be a part of the dismantling of racism and anti-Blackness. That is possible and it begins with a willingness to learn more and engage in communication that leads to better understanding—this is a very specific form of communication called **dialogue.**

Again, in my thirty plus years of teaching I have had very few students and consulting clients who have the opportunity to talk about race in ways that lead to understanding. So don't worry if you have little to no experience talking about identity differences and racial divisions—remember this Primer is designed to give you the basics to begin.

Part two of the Primer provides specific communication strategies and skills to support learning and build your capacity for, and ability to participate in, dialogue in order to:

> Dismantling racism and anti-Blackness is possible and it begins with a willingness to learn more and engage in communication that leads to better understanding—this is a very specific form of communication called **dialogue.**

- further the understanding required for shared meaning in communication across and about identity differences and racial divisions.

- affirm participant(s) in communication about and across identity differences and racial divisions and support the facilitation of shared meaning in that process.

- create opportunities to meet—across and despite divisions—in a brave space that supports humility, vulnerability, and honors humanity.

PRIMER PART ONE PROCESSING

But before you begin to think about dialogue, here are some suggestions for processing and making the most of the information presented in part one of the Primer.

1. Review where you are with the Four "Cs": The *four critical qualities you need to embrace for transformation of self and society:*

Curiosity: Did you find yourself asking questions such as:

- Why are identity differences and racial divisions so much a topic right now?

- Why are those with different racial identities treated differently and unequally?

- Why did I not know more about the backstory of race in the U.S. and globally?

- Where and how can I learn more?

- What other questions came up for you?

Courage: Did it help you to continue even when the information was difficult to hear?

- What did I feel when I encountered information that answered my questions?

- Learning new information and unlearning what we believed is challenging and uncomfortable. Did attention to courage support your learning?

- Were you mindful to resist the impulse to defend, defer or deflect?

Commitment: How or why do you find it challenging to continue this path?

- Learning more about identity and racial divisions and how to communicate about and across them is an ongoing journey. Is that daunting?

- Are you mindful of your thoughts, words, actions, and reactions daily, even minute by minute?

- Like any effort to learn something new to do different and be better reflective practice on your efforts is important part of learning. What have you been able to reflect on regularly?

Compassion: This bears repeating:

- Forgive yourself for not knowing what you were not taught.

- Unlearning and relearning is hard; offer grace to yourself on your journey.

- Offer grace to others in the process as well

- Dismantling injustice and "isms" can cause a particular form of physical and emotional fatigue because it is not easy—remember to engage in practices that can help restore your wellbeing.

2. Take some time again to check your stuff and see what you are bringing.

- As you take another look at what's in your Backstory Bag©, think about the following questions, writing down the answers so you can return to them later.

- How has the information you've read so far helped you to identify your stuff and what you bring when you are communicating about and across racial differences and identity divisions?

- What information has been difficult for you to learn?

- What information has been good for you learn?

- What would you like to learn more about?

- What resources can help you learn more? And not just asking BIPOC and others who live with marginalized identities to educate you. Have you considered:

  » written and digital sources,
  » courses you might take,
  » local community organizations you might join.

- How can you initiate the creation of a learning community of individuals who share your racial identity and want to learn more?

- What do you think you might need to support further learning as you begin the next section of the Primer with specific communication strategies for dialogue?

3. When possible, join with others committed to anti-racism work and discuss what you have learned in Part one of the Primer and how you see it influencing your communication moving forward for transformation of self and society.

PART TWO

COMMITMENT TO SUPPORT REAL TRANSFORMATION

INTRODUCTION

COMMITMENT TO SUPPORT REAL TRANSFORMATION

AS YOU CAN SEE NOW, human communication is a process—and at this time of learning more about how to be anti-racist and dismantling systemic racism, many call for "dialogue" across racial divisions. But again, is it that simple? Dialogue is not debate, dialogue begins with a commitment to better understand and when the focus is racial differences and identity divisions, understanding is not easy.

So, you ask, what's next? What now?

Yes, identity differences in the cultural context of 2023 and the communication process changes everything. A compelling example is how power is being challenged as protests call for an end to the dehumanization of Black people in the U.S., anti-Blackness, and systemic racism.

How did we get here and how can we learn in this moment, through the BLM movement, so we can finally progress? An initial step to learning more about racial discrimination, dehumanization, and anti-Blackness *is listening* as those who live it share honestly and openly about the pain of feeling targeted, dehumanized and perceived as less than. This is how dialogue begins and builds understanding that helps create that shared meaning and meeting in the middle.

But again, that warning: communication across difference, across social identities, to dialogue for better understanding is a process—and it is not easy, there are no hacks and the only aspect of that process you can really control is what you bring to the interaction.

What are you bringing to your human interactions about and across different identities and racial divisions? Ask yourself,

- How does your stuff influence your interaction with others?

- How do you navigate your stuff for interactions that affirm the humanity of the other person—and not "other" them?

- What can you let go of to help you better understand their lived experiences of social injustice?

It's important you understand that you don't have to know everything about every culture or social or racial identity—but that you make a commitment to learn more and bring that knowledge to the work you do.

- Acknowledge identity differences do exist and some matter more than others.

- Acknowledge that some ideas, experiences, and ideologies reflect privileged identities—but do not reflect *all identities.*

- Create teachable moments for yourself and your community members to learn from each other through differences.

What actions can you take to learn more about how the stuff you bring can be repacked so you can participate in transforming society?

- Where can you look?

- What can you read?

- Who can you talk to?

AND A NOTE OF CAUTION

In these recommendations to learn more, I must be clear this does not mean seeking out Black and Indigenous people of color and asking them to "teach" you about their lived experience. Learning should occur in other contexts where the burden of educating you is not placed on those who lives are impacted daily by the dehumanizing history we have just reviewed. Today, there are so many resources (some listed in the resource section) that can help you learn on your own or with a group or community of others on this journey. We will talk more about that later but for now as you begin to understand what is needed for dialogue also know that on your journey you might find those who are willing to share their experiences with you to help you understand in one-on-one interactions or in a community, and if that occurs these skills and strategies can help.

So why dialogue, why now?

Recall how you learned in the first chapter of this Primer that the communication process takes place in a cultural context. As we have previously discussed the cultural context has changed a great deal in the last sixty years with the Civil Rights Movement, second wave women's movement, LGTBQ rights movement and the recognition that public policies and laws were needed to support interpersonal actions for sustained transformation. The voices of those who were pushed out into the margins of society because they were socially constructed and perceived as less than, inferior, deviant, and dangerous are no longer silent. In the current cultural context, we now have calls for, and attempts at, dialogue across and about racial differences and identity divisions with better understanding as the goal. What might better understanding look like?

    Here is one of my favorite examples of dialogue leading to better understanding and it begins with a question: If you eat grits do you enjoy them with sugar or salt? For some people, that is a question that causes serious debate, but it has helped me to better understand why my husband Wil, might prefer sugar while I am a committed salt-on-my grits person. I associate grits with a childhood memory of cold, snowy, winter mornings and my mother at the stove watching them simmer (they stick to your ribs, she would say) as she prepared an over easy egg, (for protein, she'd remind us) before my siblings and I were allowed to go out and play in the snow. This was a warm, comforting, savory breakfast option; oatmeal was the hot cereal we ate with sugar. I never found a reason to change the flavor—so I still put salt on my grits. I have tried sugar and find it to be a taste I am certain I will never acquire.

Wil's memory of grits includes the childhood experience of traveling to Georgia every summer to visit relatives who served grits at every meal—with sugar. This was also considered a vacation even though it required he, along with other children, pick okra on the family farm—a daylong, painful task that could not be negotiated. As an adult he doesn't eat grits often, but when he does, it is with sugar. The first time we learned of our different tastes, I wanted to find out more because in my family we all used salt and I didn't know anyone who used sugar. As he shared the story of okra picking and grits with every meal, I began to understand why he might still prefer sugar. I have no desire to convert him and don't try to trick him into trying my way. That is how he likes his grits, and since I am not certain there is anywhere a policy on how to properly season and eat grits, I am not trying to get him to agree my way is the right way. Often, however, our lighthearted exchange does end like this:

Me: "SOOO, then what about shrimp and grits? That dish just begs for salt!"

His reply: "Oh, now see that is a totally different genre."

For me, this is a playful but still a great example of better understanding, but I realize some would say it is a matter of preference. So, what is the big deal? I've found it helpful to actually **hear** how his lived experience differed from mine and created our preferences.

Now I must point out here that I am in no way implying that dialogue about and across race and identity differences is about one's individual preference. I find it appalling that some people default to "we can agree to disagree" when talking about the systemic oppression and dehumanization still occurring in the twenty-first century. There is no place for "agreeing to disagree" when we are talking about the work needed to dismantle individual actions and systems that support the belief that some humans living with certain identities are more valuable or important than others. I find my grits example useful in discussing how dialogue can help lead to better understanding of why some people may hold fast to their beliefs obtained long ago in socialization—and fear the consequences of learning different information in another cultural context.

Sugar or salt? is also a reminder that the goal of dialogue is to build better understanding as a critical component in the communication outcome of shared meaning—not to win a debate. In this example the shared meaning is to enjoy our grits and there is no effort to coerce or force that enjoyment be "my way not yours." We don't assume positions of power or privilege to enact hidden agendas to make the other do something our way—we find shared meaning in "enjoy your grits."

It is important to note again that shared meaning and meeting in the middle for understanding—cannot happen if the relationship is challenged by "noise" found in the dynamics of privilege and power that are real in agent identities. Those who do something to others, have the ability to act and use privilege and power to ignore, negate or invalidate the lived experiences of another cannot build understanding so remember to: **Check yo' stuff!**

I've used the phrase "check yo' stuff" throughout the Primer and now would like to take some time and space to share an example of why I think it is important for those who want to engage in anti-racist work and social justice education needed to transform society check their "stuff." What follows is a scholarly article I wrote as a spoken word poem that reflects my feelings about calls for dialogue from people who claimed to be committed to the work but in my opinion, kept failing to actively support it. This call for dialogue across identity and racial divisions grew louder after the 2014 killing of Michael Brown in Ferguson, Missouri, a suburban community just fifteen minutes away from the campus where I'd been faculty for twenty years. Remember that I've been teaching race and communication with a focus on dialogue across divisions since the early 1990s, so when colleagues on my campus began to call for efforts to dialogue for better understanding I was encouraged, but soon dismayed by a lack of action.

I needed to vent my disappointment and frustration so I wrote *"Check yo stuff" A Black Feminist Rant to "Allies" Seeking "Dialogue" in Precarious Times* first published in 2018 in an academic journal that verified "stuff" as a scholarly word that I now use widely and often in my work. I have also performed this piece at conferences and on visits to universities where I was invited to speak and often follow the performance with the Backstory Bag© activity to allow participants the opportunity to identify the stuff they need to check if they want to be allies engaged in this important work of truth telling, dialogue, and dismantling identity divisions.

CHECK YO' STUFF

A Black Feminist Rant to "Allies" Seeking ''Dialogue" in Precarious Times

Karla D. Scott

IN THIS AGE OF BLACK LIVES MATTER, ongoing racial and social injustice protests, and the aftermath of the 2016 presidential election, there is an increase in calls from various sectors of society for dialogue—as if that particular communicative practice can magically mend divisions by reaching some form of consensus. Dialogue as a communication process holds no such promise, but the more specific communicative interaction of intergroup dialogue can move us toward shared meaning by bridging social identity divisions with understanding (Scott 2016). This process, however, requires participants show up and recognize that what they "bring" to the interaction may interfere with listening and better understanding the everyday lived experiences of marginalized and disenfranchised social identities. This "stuff" gets in the way, and checking one's "stuff" reveals what needs to be released for sharing and listening to lead to understanding and subsequent action. Yes, this is difficult work; it is more than just applauding goodwill while avoiding discomfort.

This piece emerged during a community event supported by my university. A small grassroots organization offered opportunities to dialogue across social identities, and I assumed institutional support included encouraging students, staff, and faculty to attend. But students were not there, and only a handful of "allies" from the university—those who regularly make calls to "dialogue"—showed up. As my disappointment morphed to anger, this "rant" began on a napkin from the lunch buffet.

Check yo' stuff
And I don't mean as in
Roll up curbside, push handle down, check tag is secure and hand it
to the skycap
along with a smile and tip;
then meander to gate after Starbucks stop;
settle in for peanuts, a beverage and
when again on the ground scurry to carousel
and retrieve
your stuff.
No I mean
Check yo' stuff
And not as in
a hip night out at the club,
theater,
opera,
upscale dinner with the charming young host, happy to take it,
giving you a smile and small token
with a number
so after your particular pleasure
you can retrieve
your stuff
That's right . . . I said Check yo' stuff
And not as in
my inbox
my status, bank balance, or tweets.
CHECK YO' STUFF
That's right not your literal baggage as in this airport metaphor that
I'm playing out here—
but "Yo' stuff"—that shit you carry.
Stuff that—
whether you know it or not—
guides your choices and your actions
on cute little spinning
wheels so you can move
swiftly and quickly
artfully avoiding and dodging
applauding your deft.
While ignoring how those same decisions

prevent you from
being fully present and capable of being
—an ally.
That's right
I mean open it up and
Check
It
Out!
White folks
if you want to be an ally
Unpack it
See what you got, take a good look at each piece, every bit of it.
Racism
Classism
Liberalism
Privilege
White guilt
Colonialism
Check what is still there . . . present and alive
Like a little bit of old Jim Crow tucked into the
modern-day packing cube.
Take it out
Look at it
Hold it in your hand
Turn it around
Imagine life without it
Feel the fear of letting go
The guilt of hanging on
The fear you might be left empty,
alone
vulnerable
and ashamed.
Yep,
That is why you gotta
Check it
first
before you come to the table
to dialogue—
as action

as advocate as ally.
Dialogue and truth telling in precarious times is
painful.
And
hey,
my Black folks, my people, y'all got stuff to check too
You gets
no pass
no preapproval
no priority precheck lane option here
yep you too gotta open it up
and see what's in there
Check yo' stuff
Sexism
Classism
Homophobia
Islamaphobia
Antisemitism
Shadism
And all manner of that tired old "hair" hierarchy mess
Gabby D did us Olympic proud!
Twice—you go girl!
And hey, my "allies" in the Academy
Yeah, you!
Check yo' stuff too
What you bringing?
If you think having one Black
LatinX
Muslim
Indigenous
Gay
Trans
faculty member in your department/on your campus
is progress but
have no plans for/see no need to engage them as a colleague,
support their transition to your institution,
share a meal, coffee or tea,
understand why they are hurt, angry, afraid
cuz their identity is still "out there" as "subaltern" and still not

speaking
Check yo' stuff!
And oh while I got your attention up in the Ivory Tower,
you heard me/read it right
I said yo', not "your"
It's yo'
In homage to Sista Scholar Geneva Smitherman (1986)
I have say it in the language of home
cuz when I am hurt,
when I am angry
emotions make it hard to enunciate
to comfort you as I "articulate"
Yes, know this rant resists roles imposed on us
But it is my rant to retell.
It is for us,
by us
we are Centering Ourselves
shout out to Marsha Houston and Olga Davis (2002) Some serious
Black feminist thought
Thank you Patricia Hill Collins (2009)
No mammy-ing going on here,
None at this time
We got nothing for your tears and pain, We got our own to tell round
this table right now
and this is not about you.
So while acknowledging your desire
To "dialogue"
To advocate
To process collective pain
To "coalition build" I just gotta say
Hold up,
Hang ons
Hear me out
OK?
We gon' need separate spaces for that right now.
That's right
Gather your people first, Learn as much as you can, Don't use us as
Google
But yes, you CAN Google

You can even lurk
and listen
and learn—while silent.
You can even "follow" on "multiple platforms" if you need to learn
HOW
to
check
yo'
stuff.
You can also
Read
Brenda Allen (2011)
Orbe & Harris (2015)
DuBois (1903) and Dyson (2017)
Check out the work of Lee Mun Wah (1994, 2011a, 2011b) Seek guidance from those
with experience and wisdom and strategies for understanding privilege,
responding to White guilt,
and shame
Tim Wise (2011)
Shelly Tolchuk (2010)
Brené Brown (2012)
Debby Irving (2014)
And then you might begin to understand why it's work to "stay woke."
And oh yeah
White women,
Well ya'll need a special space to check yo' stuff
—it is so deep,
maybe too deep for even the most progressive to unpack.
It needs purple gloves
for a "please step out of the line" check of yo' stuff
And I suggest you let Alice Walker's womanism guide you. (Walker, 1983)
And after you've read, listened, and learned to unpack—
then come to the table
sleeves rolled up
ready to work to "dialogue."

But know once here
We won't let you run
when you begin to squirm
in discomfort and panic
when you realize how much work dialogue requires.
I been workin' this for a quarter century now
getting folks to talk across divisions and identities
To share, and listen,
Act and do different
in daily lives,
in practice,
in policy.
And 2008 to 2016?
As Zora said—I was working like "de mule" (Hurston, 1937) to defy
outright hate of my parents' dreams of a POTUS— a dream deferred
that finally came true November 2008
And I had to work even harder
deconstructing vicious worldviews of "they" and "them" destroying
the dehumanization of "other"
dismantling walls of resistance and fear.
And then another November—2016 I wake exhausted,
in disbelief
Make America great again!
Great again?
Whose America?
Who is America?
How did this happen? much stuff was still hidden still there—
what was overcome? Why bother? Right?
This runs too deep.
The pain
the same feeling,
same fear,
same numbness and fatigue
I felt when my Mama died,
I can't breathe, I can't move,
I can't function
How do I live life now?
My life now
as me now,

there is no more me now—not the me I used to be
What now?
I been caring, carrying and totin' for 25 years,
Teaching to transform
Exhausting myself
Committed social justice warrior
And none of it mattered!
That November 2016 night
hidden in plain sight
The stuff of so many Exploded—revealing work to be done
more heavy lifting
and long hours to come
Do I have it in me?
Can I keep going?
Why should I?
I can quit!
Through my tears I see a smile
my grandbaby, my Cami-bear with her "poofy" hair,
A beautiful mass of
golden curls
that playground preschoolers often choose to berate—
While on fashion runways
grown White women emulate.
For Cami
OK
for her
I come back
But not solo this time.
No more mythical "STRONGBLACKWOMAN" (Scott 2017)
Yes, Sojourner and Harriet had allies
So come on
y'all really want to help?
Want to figure out how to reach your cousins 'cross the country?
If so, know you and your group
gotta do your own dialogue first
That is where you
Check yo' stuff
Get together
with yo' own folk first

People, please know
I honor your pain
I respect your desire,
I welcome your energy
But before you come to the table
To hear our past,
To hear our pain
To hear our plans
Check yo' stuff
Before you ask us
To share with you,
To support your efforts
to support us
To serve with you
Check yo' stuff
Before you can even begin to do work
that really unites,
You gotta know what you bringing on that path
And know that some things
Are just not needed at this table right now.
So
Check yo' stuff
So you can use your privilege for progress
So you can work better
to advocate
to liberate
and to create
coalitions
brave spaces
and peaceful places
and fight
for justice
for humanity
and love.
Cuz that's what we need from allies
in this precarious time.

So why dialogue? It can create better understanding across identity divisions

If you know little or nothing about others participating in communication in the current context it is revealed in your own communication—and shared meaning is compromised if not impossible. If you have ever asked, "How can I learn more about experiences of those living with marginalized and target, identities? Specifically, how can I learn more about anti-Blackness and systemic racism in the U.S.?" The answer is *dialogue can support that learning process.*

The late Brazilian educator Paulo Freire wrote extensively about dialogic learning theory in his book *Pedagogy of the Oppressed: Education for the Practice of Freedom*. This book is often used to further social justice education as he describes dialogue to be critical in the process. To summarize key points for this Primer, Freire stated:

1. Dialogical actions are those that promote understanding as participants share lived experiences.

2. Non-dialogic actions are those that deny validity of lived experiences, distort communication, and reproduce power.

In his description are key words we have discussed in the exploration of communication across identity differences and racial divisions: Promote understanding of the lived experiences of participants. He also notes how communication that is not dialogue can also deny and reproduce power—remember from our earlier discussions the more powerful and privileged communicator often dictates what is said, or not and who gets to tell their version of the experience and have it affirmed as true.

As we begin the exploration of dialogue it is critical to point out: **dialogue is not debate**. The goal of dialogue is not to win, to prove the other wrong, or dismiss what they share as not real because it is not your experience. Even agreement is not the goal; dialogue is designed to build a bridge to better understanding of each other, lived experiences and implications for larger society.

In this next section we will examine and practice communication strategies to support dialogue about and across racial divisions. Those strategies include:

1. listening skills,
2. language matters,
3. verbal and nonverbal communication strategies.

Our goal in this exploration is to create awareness and provide specific skills to help create and environment across various communication contexts that can help you learn and build understanding across identity differences and racial divisions.

CHAPTER FIVE
ACTIVE LISTENING

WHEN MOST PEOPLE HEAR the term communication, they think of a message being sent when someone speaks, and someone hears them. But as we know from Chapter one communication is a complicated process and sending and receiving messages by speaking and hearing is one component of that interaction. With such a belief about the process it is useful to examine more closely listening and how it can influence and interfere with creating shared meaning that leads to better understanding. In this chapter we will explore listening to offer insight as you engage in dialogue across and about social identity, racial differences, and racial divisions to develop a better understanding that will prevent "othering."

Listening is a critical skill for dialogue across and about identity differences, and racial divisions.

Why?
1. Gaining a better understanding requires active listening.
2. The reality is, however, most of the time we do not listen well.

Why?
1. Listening is a challenge.
2. Listening takes effort.

And there is a difference between hearing and listening.

1. Hearing is the physiological process of sound waves hitting the anatomy of the ear.

2. Listening is giving thoughtful attention to, making sense of, and connecting with the person. It is the "process of receiving, constructing meaning from, and responding to spoken messages" (Alberts et al., 2016, 147) it is a conscious processing of the sound waves and auditory stimuli perceived through hearing. And connecting with the person can also mean being attentive to their nonverbal communication, their gestures, posture, eye contact and voice tone.

One of the biggest communication problems is that we don't listen to understand, we listen to reply.

1. When was the last time you had to listen to better understand?

2. What did you do to listen better and show that you were actively engaged in the process?

Active listening requires you be attentive to the meaning of the sound waves hitting your ear anatomy. Even the word "active" signals you must *do something* in the process—this affirms you are not a passive participant when actively listening. When you practice active listening your presence in the process communicates that you care about the communicator, what they are sharing, and that you want to understand.

Here are some possible behaviors that can signal the absence of active listening.

- Interrupting the speaker.

- Responding vaguely, illogically, or inappropriately.

- Not looking at the speaker but rather away from them for extended periods, or across the room, or at your phone or computer screen.

It is worth noting here that engaging in physical movements as you listen can also be perceived as a lack of engagement, for example, fidgeting, foot shaking, table tapping etc. But for some individuals, engaging in physical movements such as doodling allow for more focused listening—I've had students share this as a strategy for alleviating anxiety and I've also known colleagues who knit in faculty meetings saying it relaxes them and helps them focus on what is being said. I have no reason to dispute this strategy, but I do suggest that if you find such behaviors help you to be a better listener that you find ways to intentionally communicate your presence to the one sharing—this can be done with eye contact, head nods, appropriate affirmations, and questions for example.

The following are specific listening strategies and skills for dialogue.

Listening strategies and skills.

1. Listening is holistic…it is not done just with the ears. To be actively participating you need to be fully present and engaged in the process.

2. Honor and affirm the sharing by actively listening. Do not agree to participate in dialogue to build better understanding and then not actively listen. That is an insult to the other person and the process.

3. Look at the other person, in the eyes if possible; yes, intentionally *see* them. This doesn't mean you hold an unnatural stare but a gentle gaze that centers back on the speaker if you look away.

4. Observe, and listen for, the language of their body—and yours also. What is being said? Lean in closer to be engaged.

5. Paraphrasing is an important skill in active listening. Repeat in your own words what was shared without changing the meaning or being judgmental—the aim is to show you were listening. And yes, using "what I heard

you say" is also a good way to show you are connected and care, but when you choose to use that particular phrase in the active listening process, be sure to use the speaker's own words do not paraphrase with your own.

6. Listen to what is being said **and what is not said.** If you are engaged with someone or a group for the purpose of learning more to better understand, listen for what is ***not being said or shared or validated or affirmed.***

7. Is there an "elephant in the room?" What is obvious that is being avoided? Elephants are hard to ignore so listen to what is not being said.

8. Pay attention to when you withdraw, shutdown, "fall asleep." Notice when you have disengaged. Is this because of who was speaking? Did a word or phrase or comment create some reaction that required your minds' attention?

9. Be mindful of the reality of "noise"—is it external, your own stuff, their words? Noise is very common these days, physical noise and the psychological noise of judgement, bias, and the need to jump in and say something often, anything.

10. Ask questions when you do respond—don't take it as an opportunity to make your point. See if you can get more information about what was shared. You can even preface your question with an affirmation to signal you're listening. For example: "I can imagine that was difficult for you" or "I heard you say how much that hurt." Communicate your empathy.

11. Keep breathing. Tension is normal when talking about race so notice your breath, are you holding it in anticipation of what is coming next, or what you have to say? Maintaining your breath can help you stay focused on listening—and not your own fear.

12. Silence can speak volumes. Do not rush to fill up emptiness that may occur in response to something hard to hear.

13. It is also important to remember that for individuals who identify as neurodivergent, or with certain mental health diagnoses such as attention deficit hyperactivity disorder (ADHD), anxiety, obsessive compulsive disorder (OCD) or on the Autism spectrum, fidgeting or other small repetitive movements are often helpful for focus but might be interpreted as a lack of listening by a speaker who is sharing emotions. If you are someone who identifies as neurodivergent and are engaging in active listening, it can be helpful to be mindful in your efforts to communicate and confirm that you are fully present and supportive.

LISTENING ACTIVITY

Here is an exercise in active listening to help you become familiar with what it feels and looks like. There are many versions of it with various topics as the focus but as this is a Primer about race and identity you can use that as the focus.

It requires three participants.

Identify a speaker, listener and observer.

The task is for the speaker to speak for five minutes on the questions below.

The listener only listens, no questions, or interruptions.

The observer will watch and pay attention to what is said by both speaker and listener and should take notes as they will report their observations.

1. What do you recall were communication patterns in your childhood? In your family and in your larger community? Think about specifics like who talked more, got talked over, who was silenced, who was silent, what were nonverbal messages.

   _____
   _____
   _____
   _____
   _____

2. How did that socialization influence how you communicate today?

   _____
   _____
   _____
   _____
   _____

3. What do you recall from experiences that communicated about race?

   _____
   _____
   _____
   _____
   _____

4. How did that influence how you communicate about race today—or not?

   _____
   _____
   _____
   _____
   _____

When speaker's time is up,
- Listener shares what they heard (three minutes)
- Observer shares what they saw participants doing in the interaction (three minutes)
- Speaker shares what it was like to be listened to for three uninterrupted minutes.
- Switch roles two more times so all three have participated in each role.

1. What did you notice about active listening?

   _____
   _____
   _____
   _____

2. How did it feel in your body?
   _____
   _____
   _____
   _____
   _____

3. What was difficult about it?
   _____
   _____
   _____
   _____
   _____

4. When did you find yourself shutting down, or falling asleep?
   _____
   _____
   _____
   _____
   _____

5. How often do you participate in this type of active listening in your everyday experiences?
   _____
   _____
   _____
   _____
   _____

And here is a little homework to keep you engaged on the path to improved listening:

> **In the next week, identify two contexts where you will practice active listening and record your reactions.**

CHAPTER SIX

LANGUAGE MATTERS: MICROAGGRESSIONS, AND TONE POLICING

LANGUAGE SHAPES WHAT WE SEE, know, and understand. Are you familiar with the claim that Inuit people have multiple words for different kinds of snow? I have heard that statement many times and I believe I've sometimes heard they have 14 words for snow and other times I've heard there are close to 50 words for snow. In the early 1900s anthropologists discussed the language use of Indigenous people in Artic regions and their ability to identify snow in more extensive terms than we do in English. While the reality of the claim of 50 words (more or less) for snow remains debated, what this example demonstrates is the connection between language and environment and how languages classify experiences and concepts very differently.

I have always classified snow using only a few words such as light, heavy, wet, and include phrases such as freezing rain, sleet, and ice when needed. Those words and terms are what I learned from others in my environment who understand those words as well. We keep those descriptions alive as we continue to use them with a very specific mental image and reaction when we hear "it's snowing." This is how language shapes what we see, know, and understand. I doubt I could identify other types of snow unless someone explained to me the differences so I would then be able to see and understand the implications of those differences—for example how different types of snow might influence the ability to ski well.

So, what does language use have to do with identity differences, race, and anti-Blackness? Just as the snow example illustrates, when a word is used to talk about a person or group of people an image is created in our mind and if we accept it as valid—**we act on it.** Take a moment now to, again, think about the use of "those people" and "them" you might hear often. Those words mean they are not us or like us and in our identity socialization (remember that from Chapter two) we learn we should not be like "them" because their difference is a result of deficiency or deviance, and "they" can even be dangerous. Over time a pattern develops as our perception about "them" is what we believe and in everyday lived experience is communicated.

For those living with racial identities that have been constructed as less than and dangerous, daily life is an ongoing assault of harmful, hurtful words and messages communicated through powerful systems of white supremacy and privilege that dehumanizes them. We must acknowledge the impact of the language we use to better understand how transformation can happen. In the backstory of race and racism, language has shaped the belief that Black people are less than and that people of color cannot be real citizens of the United States. Continuing to use language that supports such beliefs only serves to strengthen that perception and the racist actions that continue to occur and are justified because of that history.

"He was like a **demon** coming at me"

What image does the word demon create in your mind? This is what former Police Officer Darren Wilson said in the grand jury investigation of his killing of Michael Brown in 2014 in Ferguson, Missouri. Brown was unarmed and Wilson shot him eight times. The outrage of his killing sparked protests for days in Ferguson and across the country and energized the Black Lives Matter movement.

"Demon" is a word that creates a very specific kind of danger, and it even has religious and biblical implications as "not human." Demons need to be cast out and exorcised. If you choose to use the word demon to describe someone, it can certainly justify your need to eliminate the danger by shooting them multiple times—and even if unarmed.

Language choice is a result of our socialization where we learned about "them" as problems, trouble, threats, dangerous.

What words do you recall being used to talk about Black, Indigenous, and people of color?

> "Demon" is a word that creates a very specific kind of danger, and it even has religious and biblical implications as "not human."

CODED LANGUAGE

Coded language is using words and phrases that allow us to say something considered unacceptable but in an acceptable way, however *the intent remains the same.* I believe Wilson's use of "demon" was code for the specific sinister threat associated with Black men—or Black males of any age. This perception again is a result of centuries of messages intentionally communicating Blacks as less than human and Blacks as criminals who pose threats to society and need to be killed even when unarmed. Since Brown's death in 2014, the number of unarmed Black men and women killed by police has grown—and the response is consistently officers perceived they were in danger and had to "eliminate the threat" so the killing was justified.

Here some examples of language choices that create specific images and perceptions.

1. When Philadelphia Eagles fans celebrated their team's 2018 Superbowl win they broke storefront windows in businesses, overturned vehicles, and destroyed light fixtures and signage. They were described as exuberant—not rioters. Despite the same damage done, the words differ when used to describe the same behavior of members of a particular racial group advocating for racial justice. ***Does this sound like implicit bias perhaps?***

2. In 2004 Hurricane Katrina devastated New Orleans and many residents of the predominantly Black Ninth Ward were left without homes and access to food for days as officials worked to find suitable locations for shelters. One newspaper was criticized for the caption on a photo of two Black people wading in water with items in their hands "after looting a grocery store." Another photo with two white people wading in water included in the caption the two "found" bread and other items needed for survival. *What is the difference between "finding" and "looting"?* Some argue race.

3. Another example of coded language is: *"Make America Great Again."* Many BIPOC citizens of the United States have responded to this phrase with the question "When was it great and for whom?" This phrase demonstrates how language polarizes—and many of those who use it believe greatness was lost when the reality of the lives of women and BIPOC started to receive attention which resulted in the allocation of resources and power and eventually public policy changes that diminished the power of white supremacy. But as we have explored in this Primer, white supremacy certainly still remains a dominant force and proponents are fighting to hold onto it.

4. When armed white men and women breached the U.S. Capitol on January 6, 2021, to stop the electoral vote count, they used violence, force; some had Molotov cocktails and zip ties typically used to handcuff individuals. They chanted death threats, destroyed government property and took selfies as they trespassed in congressional members offices. The media consistently called them protestors, even though they engaged in acts of domestic terrorism. Why were they not called terrorists?

5. In the summer of 2020 when George Floyd was killed by a Minneapolis Police officer kneeling on his neck for almost nine minutes despite Floyd's pleas that he could not breathe—the Black Lives Matter movement gained more momentum across the country and world. Many news sources and social media sites shared information about the backstory of race in this country and a response I often heard from whites was: "Why are Black people trying to make us white people feel guilty?" when informed about the backstory of anti-Black racism in the United States. Their reactions weren't about the horrible history of the country, they chose to use "us and them" language that created separation and distance and even distracted the conversation from the social injustice issues being

discussed—and their realization of how they participated in them.

These are only a few examples of coded language and race and if you pay attention to what you hear—and say on any given day-- I am sure you will find examples of coded language are abundant in everyday life.

Try this for one week: make notes when you hear words that are used in place of more difficult or troubling words and that create specific negative reactions when they are used.

MICROAGGRESSIONS? WHAT ARE THEY?

Let's examine the word:
Micro = small,
Aggression = hostile violent behavior toward another; an attack,
Microaggressions = small acts of violence.

Psychology and education professor Derald Wang Sue provides a definition of microaggressions that is very specific, "everyday verbal, non-verbal, and environmental slights, snubs, or insults, whether intentional or unintentional, which communicate hostile, derogatory, or negative messages to target persons based solely upon their marginalized group membership." (Sue,2007, 3).

Microaggressions are a form of language use that reveals implicit bias and beliefs that may not even be seen as harmful. But when you experience them over and over again in your lifetime they are like a thousand paper cuts or hundreds of mosquito bites.

The term *microaggressions* was originally coined by Harvard psychiatrist Chester Pierce in the 1970s. He used it to describe ways that Black people were put down by their white counterparts. Pierce said at the time that we shouldn't look for the obvious, overt racist attacks, but rather the subtle, cumulative mini-assault. Dr. Pierce said this in 1974—and now here in the twenty-first century such subtle assaults are so frequent they are seen as normal.

Microaggressions are small acts of violence, but they add up much like a thousand paper cuts, or hundreds of mosquito bites. Yes, they are small but with so many occurring over and over again, they become cumulative and quite painful. Over the years, the concept has been extended beyond race to include similar events and experiences of other marginalized groups, including women, LGBTQ people, and people with disabilities.

Here is a statement many of my Black students have shared as a microaggression they hear often, "You're so articulate." This sounds like a compliment to be given to a Black person, right?

No—it is heard as actually meaning, "You don't talk like I think Black people should talk."

"You're so articulate" reveals your implicit bias and beliefs about the way a person who is identified as Black is supposed to speak and it also communicates your belief that all Black people talk the same and are the same.

"You're so articulate" when said by a white person to a person of color is not a compliment. This is an example of implicit bias being revealed in communication and when the speaker is made aware of the statement being motivated by racism, they will usually deny it and say, "But that is not what I meant." Intent and impact are key to understanding microaggressions. Why? Because the intention of the speaker does not lessen the impact of the pain felt when words land on the person who was the receiver.

So, comments like…

Why are all Black women so loud?
As I Black woman I hear this as I have a problem because I don't fit into the gendered concept of women as quiet, submissive, and docile.

You throw like a girl!
A young boy who hears this get the message there is something wrong with him because he is not conforming to the expectations of masculinity that demand he never do anything feminine.

I don't see color when I see you.
Yes, even though this sounds benevolent and an effort to be anti-racist, it is a microaggression. When I hear that statement I hear that you don't see the reality of my life and what I must daily confront, navigate and overcome as a Black woman. It

is hurtful to me that my race isn't important to you when it impacts my life so deeply.

Microaggressions can be so subtle that they can usually be explained away by valid reasons. This means that for recipients of a microaggression, they may find themselves asking, "What just happened here?" They might describe it as a strange feeling or sense of confusion about whether they have been attacked, disrespected, or that something is just not right. Because of this it can often be easier to handle an overt and obvious racist act than microaggressions that seem vague or disguised. But what is true is that the power of racial microaggressions to do harm is real and the use of microaggressions reveals how implicit bias is alive and functions in even the most well-meaning people.

The words you use and the messages you send matter. When you hear or encounter a microaggression, or are told what you said was hurtful or harmful to the other communicator—how can you transform or refine your own reaction (or implicit bias) so that you no longer support the belief or behavior communicating it? And please keep in mind that there is a difference between what you meant (intent) by your words and how the recipient received it (impact) illustrated in the following example:

Well intended colleague (WIC): I love everyone, we are all the same, I don't see race.
Me: But if you don't see race, then you can't see racism and you can't understand the problems and challenges, hate and violence I encounter daily because of my race.
WIC: That's not what I meant—
ME: But that is what I hear, and I want you to listen to the reality of my lived experiences and the emotional, and sometimes, physical pain that is a part of my experiences because of my race.

A takeaway from this brief, beginning discussion of microaggressions: Remember intent vs impact—how words land when we send them off does matter *and you don't get to choose how much those words weigh when they hit another person.*

Tone Policing

Tone policing is another microaggression. Tone policing is a term applied to specific verbal practices that give attention to the comfort of the privileged communicator in the interaction process while disregarding the experiences of disenfranchisement, pain, and oppression of other communicators. Typically, this occurs when the message being sent by one in a less privileged position is communicated energetically, passionately, and with much emotion about a lived experience of injustice and it gets dismissed, distorted, or devalued because the more privileged communicator prefers not to engage with and consider their own complicity. An easy "out" is to blame the tone of the speaker, blaming them for poor communication and silencing them. This allows the more privileged speaker to return to the comfort found in not having to own behavior that supports injustice.

What does tone policing sound like?
"Can you say that in a nicer way?"
"Your language is hateful and further divides us."
"This isn't the time or place for you to express your emotions."
"You need to calm down, you can't speak to me in that tone."
"I think you would have more people on your side if
you weren't so angry and rude."

There are many resources to help you learn more about microaggressions and tone policing—this brief instruction is offered to create awareness so you give attention to how your words can indeed hurt. I hope it will also keep you mindful that the journey to do different and be better is an ongoing learning process that requires a willingness to be vulnerable when admitting you do not know.

Inclusive language matters
Recall that we began this chapter talking about the connection of language use and racial differences, anti-Blackness, and identity divisions. I offered the Inuit peoples' words for snow as an example to illustrate that when a word is used an image is created in our mind and if we accept it as valid—we act on it. The same is true for the words we use to talk about people.

With any commitment to dialogue across identity divisions understanding the importance of inclusive language is critical. There is ongoing discussion and confusion about what it means and much resistance to using it. I think one of the best ways to think about the language you use when communicating about or across social identities is to choose to use terms that affirm the humanity of all individuals. What does that look like?

Below are a few examples of how language can be more affirming and inclusive. This review can provide you with information to support your own word choices and to help others understand why they might want to think about their language use as well. It is also worth noting here that this review also illustrates how language use has evolved over historical and cultural contexts to affirm the humanity of those living with identities that have been historically dehumanized and stigmatized. At the end of this discussion, I have included a resource for developing more inclusive language for race and ethnicity. This is from The Diversity Movement and the website listed in the appendix is an outstanding resource for learning more about diversity, equity, inclusivity, and affirming humanity.

SAY THIS

Black American or African American
Black refers to those whose identities are the result of an African origin even though a specific genetic analysis is not known but rather assumed from concepts such as the amount of melanin in one's skin, family history, and socio-cultural experiences. To complicate this however, you would not call someone from the Caribbean an African American because they are not from the Americas. I personally choose to identify as Black rather than African American because I have no knowledge of the African country of my ancestors and because I have several colleagues who were born in African countries and now live in the United States of America. I believe they and their children, born in the United States of America, can identify as African American in a way I cannot, yes? From their skin color others might identify them as "Black;" but let's complicate this even further. The Academy Award winning actor Charlize Theron is from South Africa and is living in America with dual citizenship, so she is African American, yes? But her skin color has always led to her racial identity referenced as white. I know it is confusing but here what I can almost guarantee is one thing: a word to never use to person whose skin color would support a racial identity of either Black or African American is the term "colored."

DO NOT SAY THIS
Colored
This is an offensive term used during legalized segregation in the United States. Earlier in the Primer, I shared images with signs indicating public spaces for "coloreds" who were forbidden to interact with white people in clearly marked "whites only" spaces. Many Black people were arrested, punished, and even killed for breaking this law that upheld the dehumanization of an entire race for decades. As discussed earlier in the Primer the use of people of color is acceptable.

SAY THIS
Undocumented immigrant
The use of undocumented immigrant reflects a process and offers an opportunity to consider reasons for seeking entry through an unauthorized process. It does not imply criminal intent.

DO NOT SAY THIS
Illegal alien
The use of Illegal alien not only dehumanizes it creates an image of a criminal who is breaking the law. There is no space to think about why they may have made such a choice to leave their own country, such as a refugee fleeing for safety. The focus is also on the individual not the act.

SAY THIS
Indigenous, Native American or refer to the specific tribe
Yes, these are terms that do not further support the subjugation and genocide of a people who were living on land in the Western hemisphere that was then "discovered" by European explorers financed for the purpose of world domination.

DO NOT SAY THIS
Indian
The use of the word Indian for Native people of the United States began when Christopher Columbus ended his Atlantic Ocean journey believing he had reached the Indian Ocean—when in fact it was the Caribbean islands. His incorrect naming of the people "Indians" was normalized when those in positions of power and privilege continued to use the term—for centuries and still today. This is an excellent example of who tells the story gets to tell the version they want believed. I grew

up hearing that was a problem from my late father who often referenced his grandmother MoMattie who was of Choctaw descent living in Mississippi—he would quote her saying: "if we'd had the guns, we would be telling the story." There are options to using a term to refer to people who were not able to keep their own names or name themselves.

SAY THIS
Enslaved people
This recognizes that those who were forced into the condition of slavery were human beings first and foremost. It affirms their humanity in a context where all efforts and actions directed at them and about them were dehumanizing.

DO NOT SAY THIS
Slave
This is a word that dehumanizes. Slavery is a condition. In any context where the word slave is used, the only image created is one whose sole purpose is to serve and service others without any attention to their own needs or wellbeing. There is no person perceived in that use and that is why it needs to be eliminated when discussing the history of people of African descent who were kidnapped and held in bondage across the globe from the sixteenth through nineteenth centuries. These were human beings.

SAY THIS
Person with a disability
This is an example of person-first language that affirms humanity by acknowledging a person is so much more than their disability.

DO NOT SAY THIS
Disabled or handicapped
This puts the focus on the level of ability a person possesses ignoring they are human.

These are just a few of the problematic terms and words you should think about letting go of in your communication about and across race and across identity differences. Words do matter as you will see in the next section.

GENDER NEUTRAL LANGUAGE

This is an area of language use where we can see the evolution, though not everyone has supported it. In the mid-twentieth century, the second wave women's movement advocated for the use of words that did not reflect only male, men, and masculinity. There are those who will still use the universal "he" and say, "well you know I mean everyone." No, the use of "he" is not inclusive of everyone which is why the terms "mailman" and "fireman" have been replaced with "mail carrier" and "firefighter" reflecting that not all in those positions are men—and one doesn't have to be a man to have such position. I admit I do cringe when I still see "mankind" used today—and I see it too often. Using "humankind" is a great way to keep reminding us that all humanity matters. And I still admire those who are trying to find a way to replace the use of "you guys" for a group because many argue "guys" is gender neutral but it is not. In homage to my family's roots in the southern United States I like to use "y'all" to refer to a group.

PRONOUN USE

As we entered the twenty-first century calls for language that is more affirming for gender identities have become louder and more prominent—again resulting in words that more accurately reflect lived experiences of those who identify their sexuality as lesbian, gay, bisexual, and their gender as transgender, queer or questioning. This is a community that again, has lived with a history of exclusion, stigma, marginalization, and hate from others, but an evolution in language use shows progress in the normalization of LGBTQ identities since the early 1990s has helped recreate more positive perceptions of the communities and those who identify with it—though we still have a long way to go.

More evidence of the power of language use in these communities is the expanding use and acceptance of pronouns to refer to individuals. Why, you might ask, do pronouns matter to an exploration of language and social identity? Once again this is about affirming humanity and gender is a social identity that is not as easy to express and live as many may believe. In many cultures, gender has been presented as an either/or binary of female/male or man/woman but there are many who do not find a place in the either/or identity. Many see their gender as more fluid in lived experiences where they express it. In some Indigenous cultures those who embrace a fluid gender identity are identified as "two-spirited" are revered and honored in the community.

Unfortunately, in many historical and cultural contexts a nonbinary gender identity expression was discouraged, forbidden, stigmatized, and in some instances even criminalized. But again, challenges to who gets to tell the story has resulted in language use that more accurately captures identity and affirms humanity.

Those in LBGTQ communities who do not identify as male or female, and use more gender expansive terms to discuss their gender use the pronouns, they/them/theirs rather than he/him/his or she/her/hers. Using the pronouns someone has indicated is a sign of respect for them and their identity by using more expansive, non-binary terms. This is an area that many communicators are learning to navigate, and if you want to learn more, there are resources in the appendix that offer more insight to support your understanding. But for purposes of the Primer, know that this inclusion of pronoun use in a section on language matters is another example of affirming humanity in communication about and across identity differences and divisions.

As we have discussed in this chapter, language shapes what we see and what we know, and words matter despite a well-known rhyme often shared in response to verbal taunts and teasing: "Sticks and stones can break my bones, but words will never hurt me." We know words do hurt. And for those living with histories of dehumanization, daily life is full of words that not only hurt when they land on them or in their lives, but they continue to inflict pain when those words are used create enduring images of them as being less than and inferior—not just different, but deficient and even deviant. Language choice is a result of a socialization where we learned about "them." Giving attention to how we might change the language we use to communicate about and across identity divisions is an important step in dialogue.

CHAPTER SEVEN

VERBAL AND NONVERBAL COMMUNICATION STRATEGIES FOR DIALOGUE

IF YOU WOULD LIKE TO HAVE a better understanding of identity differences and racial divisions and learn more about them through dialogue, then it is important you understand that the way you communicate is important. How you choose words, send and receive them, and even use silence in your messages matter in a dialogue setting whether it is with one person in an interpersonal setting or with a group of people who are choosing to learn how to talk about identity and racial divisions.

I want to include a reminder here that most white people don't have much experience talking about race in a way that leads to better understanding of the backstory of race in the U.S. or how they have contributed to racial injustices that are still common today. So please don't expect it to be easy to share and listen in a dialogue setting—either one-on-one or in a group. The following strategies can help guide you as you begin a path to know better so you can do better.

Verbal strategies for dialogue with another person

1. As you begin any dialogue about race and racial divisions, it is helpful to affirm there is difficulty in expressing

emotions that are normal when one feels vulnerable. Sharing and listening in dialogue to learn more about real life experiences with racism and anti-Blackness requires humility—the ability to admit you don't know but want to learn.

2. Ask open ended questions—the answers will provide more information and insight. An open-ended question requires more than a yes or no reply; it allows for a speaker to share more about their experiences including emotions, expectations and even pain. For example, to ask a Black person "have you encountered racism in your life?" will no doubt get you a "yes." But if you ask, "When in your life were you a target of racism and how did it affect you?—that response will give you more information about what racism looks like in various forms, and how it impacts the everyday lived experience of a Black person.

3. Validate what you hear and what is shared. For example, "John, I heard you say you first heard the N-word when you were in first grade, and it was so hard to hear the other white children laughing and pointing—it remains a vivid memory for you."

4. Be mindful of ways with words. This requires you pay attention to how language is used.

5. Critique the idea shared or the statement made—not the person making it. If someone says they believe fear of Black and Brown men is justified because they commit more crimes than white men—ask about statistics they are citing rather than saying "You are stupid and naïve to buy into stereotypes without evidence."

6. Use "I" statements to replace generalizations. "I feel uncomfortable learning specifics about the racist history of this country and how I have participated in ways I didn't even realize." Rather than: "Why are Black people always trying to make whites feel guilty?"

7. Refocus the topic if the dialogue becomes a polite discussion or debate begins. The goal of dialogue is not always agreement but better understanding. If agreeing has become the focus of communication, ask more specific questions about emotions evoked by the information shared. If winning appears to be an outcome, ask questions that might offer insight into why winning is so important it requires a devaluing of the experiences and contributions of the other communicator.

Offer compassion and extend grace. Again, sharing and listening about race, racial divisions and the pain of daily encounters with discrimination and danger is hard and there is no neat script to follow. If you are open to being a part of dialogue to help you better understand, be compassionate with yourself and others in the process. Grace is also useful in understanding that identity socialization created the long-held beliefs and behaviors that someone is now trying to release. Realizing that what you were told was harmful and hateful may require some self-reflection before relearning new ways of being and do different.

In a group where dialogue is the goal

1. As I recommended in the previous section remember to begin dialogue by acknowledging that feeling vulnerable in this process is normal for many and it can be difficult to express emotions that are normal when one feels vulnerable. Sharing and listening in dialogue to learn more about real life experiences with racism and anti-Blackness requires humility—the ability to admit you don't know but want to learn. Take time to be intentional with this affirmation—it can remind and reassure participants the goal is to learn more.

2. Create opportunities for those who don't share; draw out silent participants so they can speak. Even though some people are shy or have anxiety about talking in a group, they often feel more comfortable if space is created for them to contribute.

For example
- » "Ann, you look like you may have something to say."
- » "Rachel, I noticed you had a reaction to what Tracy said. What would you like to say?"

3. Pay attention to movement toward polarization, be aware of any "us and them" language and try to intervene by refocusing with "I" statements to replace a generalization.

4. Resist the urge to "tone police." When talking about lived experiences with social injustice, racism and anti-Blackness, anger is often common. Try not to deflect from the emotion as this is where the impact of the pain of those experiences can be understood.

5. Ask for validation and affirmation from others when the speaker indicates they are finished. It can be useful to ask another participant to perhaps "repeat one thing" they heard the speaker say. This allows for the emotion to be acknowledged and the person sharing to be affirmed and supports learning.

6. Honor silence. Yes, here it is again, silence can be useful in dialogue, so allow it to occur. Usually when there is discomfort around what is shared, it is often tempting to say something, often anything, to take the focus off what was said. Rather than rush to cover it up
   - » acknowledge the discomfort.
   - » ask participants to think about it: "Let's sit with that for a moment."
   - » model silence and don't rush to speak.

Nonverbal Strategies When You are Engaging in Dialogue with Another One on One

1. Stay mindful and alert for non-verbal reactions, or what is also known as body language. What might be communicated with:

» a frown, a grimace, or a look of exasperation,
   » shaking of head,
   » a change in posture.

2. Be mindful of what your own body language is communicating as well. Lean in to listen, use eye contact, signal to the person you are engaged in the process—and committed.

3. 3. Observe when nonverbal reactions occur and how they are a response to something shared. They are opportunities to ask questions that can draw out more information and contribute to your learning. Be aware of body language that indicates:
   » Interest
   » Confusion
   » Anger
   » Agreement
   » Withdrawing

If you are in group dialogue, below are strategies that build better understanding:

1. Try to "sweep the space" with your eyes—subtly and throughout the session. Yes, try to maintain awareness of who is participating, who is engaged, who looks like they want to say something—I call that being "preverbal."

2. Notice who talks—and who does not. It is not unusual for some to talk more than others, but you want to make sure no one dominates. This is an opportunity to create opportunities for others to contribute.

3. Race and gender privilege is one of the realities communicated in group settings. Yes, notices who talks more, who talks longer, who talks over. This is where patterns of identity socialization can be witnessed with privilege becoming very visible in those who feel entitled to speak and be heard. Recall now Vice President Kamala

Harris' calm comment in the 2020 debate when then-Vice President Pence interrupted her and started speaking over her during her two-minute allotted time: She replied, "Mr. Vice President I'm speaking."

4. Notice who reacts to what is said. Related to number three, there can be very powerful emotional responses when one is silenced or contributions are difficult to hear. This again is a place and time to be skillful and note the reaction of a participant and ask what they would like to say.

5. Recognize how tones, posture, and other nonverbal behaviors communicate the win-lose outcome of a debate.

These verbal and nonverbal strategies and skills are offered to provide you with guidance as you engage in dialogue to build better understanding. I know it would be amazing to offer a script for dialogue, but there is no way to guarantee interaction will occur in the same way each time—after all there are humans involved in this process and remember—as humans we all bring our stuff to communication. And some aren't even aware of the stuff they bring.

My goal with offering these strategies in the Primer is to provide the basics to get you started. There are many opportunities to learn more about improving communication across identity differences, engaging in difficult dialogue, building bridges to understanding, and facilitating dialogue. I have included a list of these opportunities in the appendices section. The final chapter will address what you can do with this information and how you might want to move forward on your path to learning so you can better understand, know more, do different, and do better.

CHAPTER EIGHT

WHAT NOW, WHAT NEXT? PRACTICE COMPASSION AND PROCEED WITH CARE

THE GOAL OF THE PRIMER is to help you realize that you "didn't know what you didn't know" and start you on the path to learning more. It might also be true that learning created fear—as we talked about earlier, it is a natural reaction when encountering information that challenges what we have been told and have believed for most of our lives. Cognitive dissonance is the psychological term for a response where we try to make sense of information that contradicts and challenges our comfort. It can certainly take time and effort to move through that discomfort to accept and embrace a new way of not just believing, but of being. It might be useful to reflect on the emotions that have come up for you in the activity here—remember to proceed with compassion and face fear, committing to be courageous.

> Without fear, we are able to see more clearly our connections to others. Without fear, we have more room for understanding and compassion. Without fear we are truly free.
> —Thich Nhat Hanh

EMOTIONAL REFLECTION

Excellent resources for working through difficult emotions are *Rising Strong* by Brené Brown (or any of her books on emotional vulnerability), and *Witnessing Whiteness* by Shelly Tochluk.

1. What came up as you read the Primer and completed the activities? Anger, fear, guilt, shame? All of these are

common responses to encountering new information that challenges our beliefs and behaviors.

_____
_____
_____
_____
_____

2. In what areas did you find you needed **courage** to keep going?

_____
_____
_____
_____
_____

3. What did you do with any fear encountered as you worked through the Primer? Have you found a way to embrace it and work through it?

_____
_____
_____
_____
_____

4. What other time in your life can you recall where you had to give up a belief or behavior after you received new information that contradicted what you had long embraced as good (or really not that bad) for you? For instance, quitting smoking, adopting different diet and nutrition choices, becoming more physically active, or ending an unhealthy relationship. What helped you move through this time?

_____
_____
_____
_____
_____

5. Where can you find others to join you on your journey of social justice education to learn more and do different? Remember, community support can be useful when walking an unknown path.

   _____
   _____
   _____
   _____
   _____

6. What resources do you have to help you navigate emotions arising from this work? Remember, realizing what you didn't know can be hard to hear. If you need professional help to support and restore your wellbeing—please seek it out.

   _____
   _____
   _____
   _____
   _____

I developed this Primer for those who are interested in learning how to communicate about racial differences and across identity divisions in social justice work intended to dismantle racism and anti-Blackness in the United States to create a new normal centering and honoring humanity—resulting in that "liberty and justice" for all—for real, for real. My hope is that people from all walks of life, everyday folks who want to do better will find it useful as they commit to go forward and keep learning either on your own or in a group.

I would like to think professionals in social work, mental health, legal services, health care and all levels of education will find it especially useful as a starting point for self, colleagues and organizations to do better. I consider myself a "teacher-scholar" and so will always have a soft spot for sharing this information with educators, because they can plant seeds that sprout, grow out, go out, and sustain change. But I remain disappointed that so many teacher training curricula are not intentional in building capacity to understand "how we got here" and improve communication about and across racial divisions in their professional contexts. It is also sad that in 2021 many states began outlawing educational materials that focus on dismantling social identity divisions and dehumanization and banning books that reveal what lived experiences look like so learning can occur across those divisions. I firmly believe these actions and such mandates are motivated by fear and further fuels my desire to make the critical information that I share in this Primer accessible so all can better understand "how we got here." I do hope teachers at all levels of educational institutions find this Primer of use.

Others who can greatly benefit are employed in human service agencies, are community workers and religious leaders—those who are often in nonprofit organizations designed to help, problem solve and offer support to those living with consequences of oppressive systems that dehumanize identities including structural racism, and anti-Blackness. But this does not mean employees of for-profit businesses, organizations and even Fortune 500 companies won't find it useful. I think anyone, in any position can benefit from the opportunity to learn what has been omitted in our personal backstory of race, society's backstory of race and what has contributed to "how we got here" as a country.

I also believe the Primer can be useful for organizational change as well, in eliminating the systemic racism and oppressive structures of exclusion that have become "just the way things are" in the corporate world. I believe the lack of this information in college courses throughout most of the twentieth century is the reason so many people believe "the way things are" should remain the status quo regardless of who is disenfranchised and disadvantaged. But it is time to change that belief and many universities now require students take classes that offer a broader understanding of identity, race, privilege, and power in the U.S.

Yes! And that is great, but for those who graduated years, even decades ago and have no reason to be in a college classroom today, I offer the Primer with the basic elements needed to start and support better understanding. This is for anyone who wants to learn. Lifelong learning is the key—so my hope is that you will seek out more resources to help you understand more beyond what you received in this Primer. I suggest you find community to support you because there are others looking to better understand as well; others who want to learn more so they can do different.

What if you are interested in individual and institutional transformation?

One of the goals of this Primer with specific information is to *build your capacity* to engage in dialogue and communicate about and across racial identity differences and divisions.

I do want you to know, however, that this understanding and knowledge is also critical to institutional transformation, the real change that dismantles inequality, systemic oppression, and anti-Blackness leading to a more diverse, equitable and inclusive organization. Yes, the goal is to build *your* capacity, but if you are an employee, administrative leader, or board member of an organization committed to change, you can share what you've learned in the Primer and contribute information and strategies to support your organization's plan to becoming more diverse, equitable, and inclusive.

What can you do as an employee or community member? Here are a few suggestions.

1. Encourage and model the desire to engage in learning that leads to understanding and requires deep personal sharing—and humility. This is not easy and as I hope you have learned, there are no hacks so:
   » Be prepared to stay with dialogue that leads to better understanding.
   » Be honest—with yourself and your colleagues—about your "why" for beginning the journey and why it is hard.
   » Utilize resources to help you and your colleagues in the journey. There are many books and documentaries available, a few are listed in the appendices.

2. In addition to practicing communication strategies to increase understanding and support on a path to transforming the organization or community, keep in mind the reality of target and agent groups—just look at who gets more attention and benefits and *how that is communicated*:
   » Who gets hired, mentored, rewarded, promoted?
   » Which ideas, proposals, projects are validated?
   » Who gets included in formal and informal meetings?

- » Ask yourself what is the message communicated in those actions: "*Some of you are clearly more important than others so enjoy the privileges of it.*"
- » Take a look around the organization or community group and think about this: *How has privilege created and supported the current representation?*

I LEAVE YOU WITH THIS THOUGHT

How can your communication interrupt and intervene in ways that help dismantle systematic racism, anti-Blackness and "othering" in your own family, communities, workplace, larger society, and even globally?

This change can feel overwhelming and intimidating—some actions may feel and be beyond your control. There are, however, individual efforts are you can control:

1. What you bring.

2. How you communicate about and across racial differences and identity divisions.

3. How you can resist participating in oppressive, racist systems that target people living with identities that have been stigmatized, marginalized, and dehumanized.

No matter the communication context, dialogue about and across identity differences and racial divisions offers an opportunity to support understanding that leads to the real action needed for real change and transformation.

In closing, I offer a reminder as you embrace the information in the Primer and begin your journey to do better. The work is hard, be compassionate with yourself, and *engage in restorative practices that can help create and support your emotional, mental, and physical wellbeing.* Also seek out professional help and support to navigate feelings that might arise from encountering information that might be hard for you to hear.

I think it is also wise to "choose your challenges"—not everyone will want to hear or participate in the journey you have begun. Not everyone in your family, community, or circle of friends will share your commitment to better understand, facilitate, and transform—to try to educate them to join you may take more time and effort than you have available. You should decide where, and how, to direct your energy; remembering to extend grace and be willing to let go of a need to prove, save, or caretake.

And finally, another reminder to revisit and re-embrace the Four "Cs."

**CURIOSITY,
COURAGE,
COMMITMENT,
AND COMPASSION.**

Continue to welcome **curiosity,** asking questions such as:

1. Why are identity differences and racial divisions so much a topic right now?

2. Why are those with different racial identities treated differently and unequally?

3. How can I better understand the experiences of those who live with identities different than mine?

4. Why did I not know more about the backstory of race in the U.S. and globally?

5. Where and how can I learn more?

Remain **courageous** as you continue even when the going gets rough.

1. What am I feeling when I encounter information that answers my questions?

2. Learning new information and unlearning what we believed is challenging and uncomfortable.

3. When you feel what you identify as fear, acknowledge it, exhale, and as bravely and gently as you can, walk through it.

Commit and re commit often, maybe even daily

1. Remember learning more about identity and racial divisions and how to communicate about and across them is an ongoing journey.

2. You must be mindful of your thoughts, words, actions, and reactions daily, even minute by minute.

3. Like any effort to learn something new to do different and be better, reflective practice on your efforts is important part of that process.

May **compassion** become your constant companion

1. Forgive yourself for not knowing what you were not taught.

2. Unlearning and relearning is hard; offer grace to yourself on you journey.

3. Offer grace to others in the process as well.

4. Dismantling injustice and "isms" can cause a particular form of fatigue, restorative practices can support and sustain you. This is not always easy work and if you exhaust yourself trying to learn everything at once or engage in multiple opportunities to learn to relieve guilt, you can burnout, and that will only contribute to a sense of resignation that it is all too much. Remember to offer compassion to others and resist the need to fight to change or "save" them if they are committed to remaining where they are.

I know that for many, this journey will not be easy to start, but I hope the information you have found in this Primer propels you to go forward.

In closing, I share these words from Rolf Gates, one of my favorite yogis:

> *Insight is the human capacity to see outside of our conditioned way of seeing; it is literally the ability to see what we are in the habit of not seeing. It is a natural capacity that we all share, as is the ability to put it to work in our lives…Putting insight into practice takes courage…a new insight into how to live means the first time we act according to a new insight we will have had zero practice with it. Not only are we new to whatever choices our insight is inviting us to make, our friends and family are new to it as well. To make matters worse insight always involves love and the actions that we take to express love.*
>
> (Gates 2015, p.39)

My friend, colleague, and former student Peter Ershen and I are honored to leave you with this original collaborative piece to inspire you further on your journey.

> *I didn't know what I didn't know; I believed what I was told*
> *Seeing the truth so clearly is challenging work*
> *When you must release the old.*
> *There's nothing to fear, that past led us here*
> *So listen to what's new and be brave*
> *Nurturing the courage to change my mind.*
> *Is the path toward more hopeful days*
> *There is so much more I need to learn to replace*
> *what I thought was right.*
> *But I'll communicate commitment everyday of my life*
> *Transformed by this insight.*
> *KDS & PE*

BIBLIOGRAPHY

Alberts, Jess K., Thomas K Nakayama, and Judith Martin. *Human Communication in Society*. Boston, MA: Person, 2016.

Allen, Brenda J. *Difference Matters: Communicating Social Identity*. Long Grove, IL: Waveland, Press, 2011.

Brown, Brené. *Daring Greatly: How the Courage to be Vulnerable Transforms the Way We Live, Love, Parent, and Lead*. New York, NY: Avery, 2012.

Collins, Patricia Hill. *Black Feminist Thought: Knowledge, Consciousness, and the Politics of Empowerment*. New York: Routledge, 2008.

Dubois, W.E.B. *The Souls of Black Folk*. Chicago, IL: A.C. McClurg, 1903.

Dyson, Michael Eric. *The Tears We Cannot Stop: A Sermon to White America*. New York, NY: St. Martin's Press, 2017.

Freire, Paulo. *Pedagogy of the Oppressed*. New York, NY: Herder & Herder, 1970.

Frye, Marilyn. *The Politics of Reality: Essays in Feminist Theory*. Berkeley, CA: Crossing Press, 1983.

Gates, Rolf. *Meditations on intention and being: Daily reflections on the path of yoga, mindfulness and compassion*. Anchor Books 2015.

Harro, Bobbie. "The Cycle of Socialization." In *Readings for Diversity and Social Justice*, edited by Maurianne Adams, Warren Blumenfeld, Carmelita Rosie Castañeda, Heather W. Hackman, Madeline L. Peters, and Ximena Zúñiga, New York, NY: Routledge, 2000.

Houston, Marsha, and Olga Idriss Davis, eds. *Centering Ourselves: African American Feminist and Womanist Studies of Discourse* Cresskill, NJ: Hampton Press, 2002.

Hurston, Zora Neale. *Their Eyes Were Watching God*. New York, NY: Lippincott & Co., 1937.

Irving, Debbie. *Waking Up White: And Finding Myself in the Story of Race*. Cambridge, MA: Elephant Room Press, 2014.

Mun Wah, Lee, producer and director. *The Color of Fear*. Stir Fry Seminars and Consulting, Inc., 1994.

Mun Wah, Lee, producer and director, *If These Halls Could Talk*. Stir Fry Seminars and Consulting, Inc., 2011.

Mun Wah, Lee. *Let's Get Real: What People of Color Can't Say and Whites Won't Ask About Racism*. Berkeley, CA: Stir Fry Seminars and Consulting, Inc., 2011.

Orbe, Mark P. *Constructing Co-Cultural Theory: An Explication of Culture, Power, and Communication*. Thousand Oaks, CA: SAGE Publications, 1998.

Orbe, Mark P. *Communication Realities in a "Post Racial Society:" What the U.S. Public Really Thinks About Barack Obama*. Lanham, MD: Lexington Books, 2011.

Orbe, Mark P., and Tina M Harris. *Interracial Communication: Theory Into Practice*. Thousand Oaks, CA: Sage Publications, 2015.

Saad, Layla. *Me and White Supremacy: Combat Racism, Change the World, and Become a Good Ancestor*. Naperville, IL: Sourcebook Publishing, 2020.

Smitherman, Geneva. *Talkin and Testifyin: The Language of Black America*. Detroit, MI: Wayne State University Press, 1986.

Stewart, John. *Bridges Not Walls: A Book About Interpersonal Communication*. New York, NY: Random House USA, 1986.

Sue, Derald Wing, Christina M. Capodilupo, Gina C. Torino, Jennifer M. Bucceri, Aisha M.B. Holder, Kevin L. Nadal, and Marta Esquilin. "Racial Microaggressions in Everday Life: Implications for Clinical Practice." *American Psychologist* 62, no. 4 (2007): 271–86.

Tochluk, Shelly. *Whitnessing Whiteness: The Need to Talk About Race and How to Do it*. Lanham, MD: Rowman & Littlefield, 2010.

Walker, Alice. *In Search of Our Mathers Gardens*. New York, NY: Harcourt Brace, 1983.

Wise, Tim. *White Like Me: Notes From a Privileged Son*. Berkeley, CA: Soft Skull Press, 2011.

RESOURCES
FOR FURTHER LEARNING ON YOUR JOURNEY

BOOKS

Allan Johnson
Privilege, Power and Difference
https://www.agjohnson.us/books/privilege/

Layla Saad
Me and White Supremacy
https://www.meandwhitesupremacybook.com

Thomas DeWolf, Jodie Geddes
The Little Book of Racial Healing
https://www.skyhorsepublishing.com/9781680993622/the-little-book-of-racial-healing/

Carol Anderson
White Rage: The unspoken truth of our racial divide
https://www.bloomsbury.com/us/white-rage-9781632864123/

Debby Irving
Waking up White: And finding myself in the story of race
https://debbyirving.com/the-book/

Robin DiAngelo
White fragility: Why it's so hard for White people to talk about racism
https://robindiangelo.com/publications/

Derald Wing Sue
Race talk and the conspiracy of silence: Understanding and facilitating difficult dialogues on race
https://www.wiley.com/en-us/Race+Talk+and+the+Conspiracy+of+Silence%3A+Understanding+and+Facilitating+Difficult+Dialogues+on+Race-p-9781119241980

Ijeoma Oluo
So you want to talk about race?
https://www.sealpress.com/titles/ijeoma-oluo/so-you-want-to-talk-about-race/9781580056779/

Shelley Tochluk
Witnessing Whiteness: The need to talk about race and how to do it
http://witnessingwhiteness.com

Rhonda Magee
The Inner Work of Social Justice: Healing ourselves and transforming our communities through mindfulness
https://www.rhondavmagee.com

Annellese A. Singh
The Racial Healing Handbook: Practical activities to help you challenge privilege, confront systemic racism and engage in collective healing
https://www.newharbinger.com/racial-healing-handbook

Beverly Daniel Tatum
Why are all the Black kids sitting together in the cafeteria? And other conversations about race. Twentieth anniversary edition.
https://www.beverlydanieltatum.com

Tochluk Shelly
Witnessing Whiteness: The Journey into Racial Awareness and Antiracist Action 3rd ed.
Lanham, MD: Rowman & Littlefield.

RESOURCES FOR VIEWING AND DISCUSSING RACE AND SOCIAL JUSTICE

Nicole Hannah-Jones
https://nikolehannahjones.com

The 1619 Project
https://www.nytimes.com/interactive/2019/08/14/magazine/1619-america-slavery.html
BOOK: *The 1619 Project A New Horizon* by Nicole Hannah-Jones

Bryan Stevenson
Equal Justice Initiative
https://eji.org/bryan-stevenson/
https://eji.org/projects/true-justice/

Just Mercy
Movie
https://www.youtube.com/watch?v=GVQbeG5yW78
BOOK: https://www.amazon.com/Just-Mercy-Story-Justice-Redemption/dp/081298496X

Ava DuVernay

DOCUMENTARY: 13th

https://www.google.com/search?client=safari&rls=en&q=ava+duvernay+13th+trailer&ie=UTF-8&oe=UTF-8

Immigration Nation

https://www.youtube.com/watch?v=X_xVKy58Yuw

RACE: The Power of an Illusion

https://www.racepowerofanillusion.org

James Baldwin

I am not your Negro

https://www.youtube.com/watch?v=rNUYdgIyaPM

Jane Elliot

https://janeelliott.com

Tema Okun

White identity Ladder

https://www.dismantlingracism.org/uploads/4/3/5/7/43579015/okun_-_white_sup_culture.pdf

Tema Okun

White supremacy culture: Coming home to who we really are

https://www.whitesupremacyculture.info

WEBSITES

Breaking the prejudice habit
http://breakingprejudice.org

ACKNOWLEDGMENTS

My gratitude for this work begins with my late parents, Doris and Travis Scott, and their determination that their children have a good education. That commitment resulted in me transferring in 4th grade to an all-white Lutheran grade school in an all-white town one hour away from my home. During those five years as I learned the "3Rs" I also learned much about race, racism, and cultural border crossing—literally and figuratively. I learned to negotiate identity and think about the implications of actions and language in the very different worlds of my all-Black neighborhood and all-white school community. I believe that skill led me to this path on my journey as "teacher-scholar."

I am forever grateful the faculty in my communication master's program at Southern Illinois University at Edwardsville where the "hippies who taught me to teach" also taught me to care for my students as much as the curriculum. Thank you, Pat Goehe (RIP). In 1990, I co-taught my first Race and Communication class at SIUE in a one-week workshop with 50 students across race, age, gender, social economic class, and religion and it was there I witnessed the value of creating a brave space where being vulnerable while sharing and listening about lived experiences supported learning across those identity differences and divisions. That first experience inspired me to 'teach to transform' and later in my doctoral program I found ways to further examine communication across differences to bridge racial divisions. In my decades as faculty at Saint Louis University, a Catholic Jesuit university with a mission to "transform society," I was able to live that commitment and walk that path! Thank you, SLU.

So many of my students have inspired me and have gone forward to continue the teaching, learning, disruption, and dismantling that will transform—there are far too many to thank here but you know who you are out there "doing the darn thing" and "setting the world on fire." Three of those students read versions of the Primer offering feedback and editing expertise—thank you Peter Erschen, Deborah Macey, and Kerry Wilson. To my colleagues across the academy who have created a courageous community conspiring to keep the humanization, equity, inclusion, and affirmation of all identities at the center of what we do—I appreciate you and am honored to be among a group of shoulders on which the next generation stands!

Along this path I also encountered activists, allies, and advocates who live their commitment to anti-racism out loud every day with courage and vulnerability. Many of them are cohort members from my Stir Fry Seminars Mindful Dialogue Facilitation programs who continue to inspire me; this work honors all you do—and much love to you Lee Mun Wah. A special shout out to Gabriel Kram for critical conversations on the path to publication and the introduction to Kevin Barret Kane for the beautiful design—thank you both for grace and guidance. My talented niece and goddaughter Jasmine Wright, thank you for sharing another of your gifts with the creation of the bridge image for the cover.

To colleagues, associates, and friends who created contexts for me to share this curriculum in presentations, professional development opportunities, and trainings at your institution or organization thank you for support and for believing that transformation is possible. I was fortunate to find one special group living that belief and I owe them a huge hug of gratitude. The "old white hippies" of Yachats, Oregon standing along Highway 101 in solidarity with the Black Lives Matter movement and demanding social justice, thank you for encouraging me to complete this work. My dear friend Cheris, I offer you a bow of gratitude for many years of mentoring and love—to you and Dale a special thanks for the perfect place in the "Scholar's Room" to write at the coast!

I must also thank my immediate and extended family, past and present, whose faces reflect the history of our lineage in a range of skin tones and melanin, revealing stories of "passing" and fleeing violence in the Jim Crow south for opportunity in the "Promised Land" of the north. Our 20th century ancestors crossed cultural borders, navigated identities, and demonstrated against dehumanization, believing that we—their children, and their children's children—would live in a world where our identities and humanity would be valued and affirmed in all forms of interaction and communication. It is with a deep bow of gratitude to them and that legacy I offer work I believe can help build bridges to the better understanding that will transform society.

ABOUT THE AUTHOR

Karla D. Scott is a proud native of East St. Louis, Illinois where she enjoyed her first career as a journalist before pursuing graduate study and completing her doctorate in communication and culture at the University of Illinois Urbana-Champaign. She joined the faculty of the Department of Communication at Saint Louis University in 1994 and is the first Black woman faculty member to be hired at Saint Louis University at the academic rank of Assistant Professor, tenured and promoted to the rank of Associate Professor, and subsequently promoted to Full Professor. During her time at SLU, she served as Director of African American Studies, growing the program from an interdisciplinary certificate program to an academic major, and served as the first Assistant Dean for Diversity and Inclusion in the College of Arts & Sciences.

She is an award-winning teacher and researcher and developed the university's first Intergroup Dialogue initiative with a curriculum to build capacity to communicate about and across identity differences. She is also the author of *The Language of Strong Black Womanhood: Myths, Models, Messages, and a New Mandate for Self Care* published by Rowman & Littlefield. Beyond the university she shares her passion for communication as a path for transformation through her consulting practice, Dialogue, Diversity & Dharma, LLC and is also a 200-hour Certified Yoga Teacher. She remains close to her hometown on the bluffs of southern Illinois sharing a home with her husband wonderful Wil and pandemic puppy Frida.

Learn more about her work at
www.drkarladscott.com

www.ingramcontent.com/pod-product-compliance
Ingram Content Group UK Ltd.
Pitfield, Milton Keynes, MK11 3LW, UK
UKHW061203180426
11947UKWH00031B/2066